CRAWSHAW'S
SKETCHING & DRAWING
COURSE

CRAWSHAW'S SKETCHING & DRAWING COURSE

ALWYN CRAWSHAW

HarperCollins*Publishers*

in association with
Channel Four Television Corporation
and J. R. Productions

First published in 1995 by
HarperCollins Publishers, London

© Alwyn Crawshaw, 1995

Designed, edited and typeset by Flicka Lister
Design assistance: Susan Howe
Photography: Nigel Cheffers-Heard
Location photography: Liam Furlong
Map of Bahamas: Valerie Hill

**A catalogue record for this book is available
from the British Library**

ISBN 0 00 412791 9
Printed and bound in the UK

ACKNOWLEDGEMENTS

June and I would like to record our sincere
thanks to Cathy Gosling from HarperCollins,
to Flicka Lister for designing and editing
this book, and also to Mary Poole for typing
the manuscript.

We would also like to thank our producer,
David John Hare, and all the members of the
television crew for their tremendous support
and patience during the making of the
television series.

Finally, we would like to express our gratitude
to the Bahamas Tourist Office and to the
wonderful people of the Bahamas for the help
and kindness they showed us during our stay.

The 10-part television series, *Crawshaw's
Sketching & Drawing Course*, was produced and
directed by David John Hare of J. R. Productions
for Channel Four. Videos of the series are
available from Teaching Art Ltd, PO Box 50,
Newark, Nottingham NG23 5GY; telephone
01949 844050.

CONTENTS

ABOUT THE ARTISTS

ALWYN CRAWSHAW

Successful painter, author and teacher Alwyn Crawshaw was born at Mirfield, Yorkshire, and studied at Hastings School of Art. He now lives in Dawlish, Devon, with his wife June, where they have their own gallery.

Alwyn works in watercolour, oils, acrylics and occasionally pastels. He is a fellow of the Royal Society of Arts, and a member of the Society of Equestrian Artists and the British Watercolour Society. Alwyn is also President of The National Acrylic Painters Association.

Alwyn's best-selling book *A Brush with Art* accompanied his first 12-part Channel Four television series in 1991, followed by *Crawshaw Paints on Holiday*, *Crawshaw Paints Oils*, *Crawshaw's Watercolour Studio* and *Crawshaw Paints Acrylics*, all with tie-in books of the same titles. This book, *Crawshaw's Sketching and Drawing Course*, accompanies his sixth Channel Four television series.

Alwyn's books for HarperCollins include eight in their *Learn to Paint* series, *The Artist at Work* (an autobiography of his painting career), *Sketching with Alwyn Crawshaw*, *The Half-Hour Painter*, *Alwyn Crawshaw's Watercolour Painting Course*, *Alwyn Crawshaw's Oil Painting Course* and *Alwyn Crawshaw's Acrylic Painting Course*.

Alwyn has been a guest on local and national radio programmes, including *The Gay Byrne Radio Show* in Eire, and has appeared on various television programmes. Alwyn has made several successful videos on painting and in 1991 was listed as one of the top ten artist video teachers in America. He is also a regular contributor to *Leisure Painter* magazine.

Alwyn organizes his own successful and very popular painting courses and holidays, as well as giving demonstrations and lectures to art groups and societies throughout Britain. In 1992, he co-founded the Society of Amateur Artists, of which he is President. Alwyn has exhibited at the Royal Society of British Artists in London and he is listed in the current edition of *Who's Who in Art*.

Painted mainly from nature and still life, Alwyn's work has been favourably reviewed by critics. *The Telegraph Weekend Magazine* reported him to be 'a landscape painter of considerable expertise' and the *Artists and Illustrators* magazine described him as 'outspoken about the importance of maintaining traditional values in the teaching of art.'

JUNE CRAWSHAW

Surrey-born June Crawshaw started her artistic career mainly as a potter. From 1980, she concentrated her creative talents on painting and continued to develop her own individual style of watercolour painting.

June now paints in watercolour, acrylics, oils and occasionally pastels. She is a member of the Society of Women Artists and a member of the British Watercolour Society. June is also listed in the current edition of *Who's Who in Art*.

June has been a guest on radio programmes and is contributor to *Leisure Painter* magazine. For the last ten years, she has taught with Alwyn on his residential painting courses, as well as painting alongside him in his previous television series *Crawshaw Paints on Holiday* and *Crawshaw Paints Acrylics*. Her work is included in the tie-in books of the same titles. June's first book, *Watercolour Made Easy*, was published by HarperCollins in 1995.

Original work by June may be found in collections throughout the UK and abroad. She exhibits her work in galleries in the UK and also at The Crawshaw Gallery in Dawlish.

INTRODUCTION

Over the past five years, I have made five television series. My wife June, who is also an artist, helped me off camera in three of these series and was featured painting alongside me in *Crawshaw Paints On Holiday*, filmed in Majorca in 1992. In my last television series, *Crawshaw Paints Acrylics*, filmed in County Kerry in southern Ireland in 1994, she took a more prominent part. Since then, it seems very natural for June to be part of my television programmes, and we were delighted to be teamed together again for *Crawshaw's Sketching & Drawing Course*.

For this series, we were invited by the Bahamas Tourist Office to film in their country. Although there are over 700 islands in the Bahamas, we filmed in just two: Harbour Island and New Providence Island, where the capital and chief port of Nassau is situated. Many people have told us that they enjoy following in our footsteps to find and paint scenes that we have used on television. If you ever have the chance to visit the beautiful and inspiring islands of the Bahamas, there is some useful information on

page 128 to help you and I know you will have a wonderful time, just as we did.

In my previous television series, I concentrated on painting in watercolour, oils or acrylics. Most of the drawing was done off camera, and a sequence would start with me saying, 'Now the drawing is done, let's start painting'. This is fine when you are demonstrating painting techniques, but we have had many requests to make a series on sketching. So, after discussion with our television producer, David Hare, it was decided to make a series on sketching and drawing.

I decided that the main emphasis should be on sketching because this doesn't sound too frightening to the beginner. However, the television programmes also provide plenty of basic drawing tuition to help beginners on their way and this book contains additional teaching instruction.

The ten programmes in the television series offer a progressive teaching course and this book follows the same sequence, enabling you to study and work through the lessons in your own time. Please copy our sketches, if you wish. This will help you to gain confidence, especially for working outdoors.

THE THREE-MINUTE SKETCH

One very important feature included in most of the programmes are our 'three-minute sketches'. Completing a sketch in just three minutes may sound rather nerve-racking but don't worry. If you have a pencil and paper handy, time yourself for three minutes and just cover the paper with scribbled pencil lines. You'll be amazed at how many lines you can draw in the time. Once you know where and how to draw those lines, they will make sense and you will be able to create a good sketch.

To be able to sketch or draw successfully, you must concentrate your whole mind on your subject matter and really observe – not just look casually – so you know exactly where to draw your pencil lines. You will learn more about observation in Programme 8. You also need to know how to simplify the drawing of your subject and to pick out the important elements without being tempted to fiddle. The three-minute sketch will help you to develop these skills quickly and is therefore a very useful exercise. June and I still do them when we are out sketching since we need to sharpen our skills in the same way as anyone else, even though we have a lot of experience behind us. If your attempts look awkward at first, don't worry. You will be learning something every time you try.

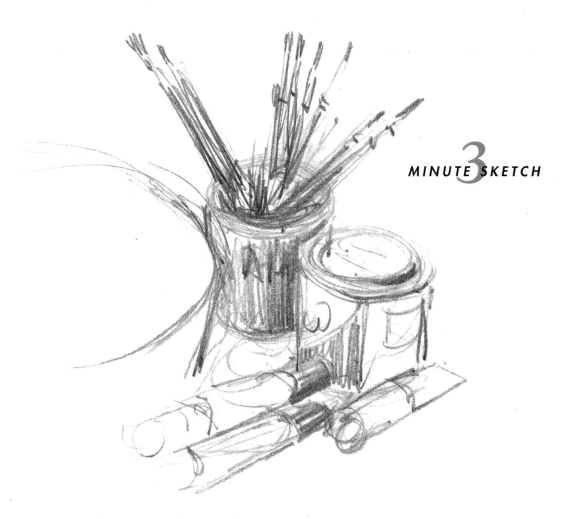

MINUTE 3 SKETCH

Brushes, 2B pencil on cartridge paper, 25 × 17 cm (10 × 7 in)

1

ABOUT SKETCHING

If you have friends who paint, I am sure you will have heard them say about a painting they have done, 'Oh, that's just a sketch'. What they are really saying is that they aren't very happy with the painting. Early in my painting career, I used the same excuse! But, of course, this has nothing at all to do with sketching. A sketch is a creative work of art in its own right, not a poor painting. In fact, some people prefer the sketches of the famous landscape artist John Constable to his finished studio paintings.

The sketch can be divided into three categories: an information sketch; an atmosphere sketch; and, finally, an enjoyment sketch. But remember that all three forms of sketching will teach you how to draw and paint.

INFORMATION SKETCHES

These sketches are used for gathering information to paint from later at home or in the studio. I normally use pencil for this type of sketch because it enables me to work quickly and pencil is also good for drawing detail.

While we are on the subject of sketching outdoors, whether you are standing up or sitting down, don't try to work doing a balancing act! For complete control of your painting arm and hand, the rest of your body must be well-balanced and comfortable. Naturally, there are times when, just to be able to see your subject, you need to be in an uncomfortable position. This is acceptable, but try not to make a habit of it.

Information sketch, *Boats at Plymouth Hoe*, 2B pencil on cartridge paper, 20 × 28 cm (8 × 11 in)

Information sketch, *Exmouth*, 2B pencil on cartridge paper, 28 × 40 cm (11 × 16 in)

I did the quick pencil sketch (left) because I wanted to gather information about different craft at Plymouth Sound in Devon. If I had wanted the boats in detail, I would have observed them much closer and at anchor and, of course, I would have taken a lot longer to sketch them.

I did the information pencil sketch (above) many years ago at Exmouth Harbour in Devon. I have done watercolour, oil and acrylic paintings of various sizes, over the years, from this sketch. This shows the value of a good information sketch.

I didn't draw any sky in this sketch, simply because I didn't need it. Whenever I have used it I have 'created' my own sky. If, when I drew the sketch, I had been inspired by a dark, ominous, stormy sky behind the light-coloured buildings, I would have shaded the dark sky in.

June drew the information sketch (right) when we were in Majorca. She wasn't concerned about the olive trees in the foreground, except for their position in the scene. The information she wanted to capture was the buildings showing above the olive grove, the skyline with cypress trees and the distant houses.

If you have a camera with you, take a photograph of your scene as well. This will help you with particular references when you paint from your sketch back at home.

Information sketch, *Fornalutx, Majorca*, 2B pencil on cartridge paper, 20 × 12.5 cm (8 × 5 in)

Atmosphere sketch, *River Wey, Surrey*, 2B pencil on cartridge paper, 28 × 40 cm (11 × 16 in)

ATMOSPHERE SKETCHES

You can see that I have put very little detail into either of the two atmosphere sketches on this page. The sketch (above) shows the shape and form of the 'full' summer trees and also the shape and strength of the reflections in the river. I achieved this with very free but positive strokes of my 2B pencil. For me, this sketch brings back the memory and atmosphere of a hot midsummer's day by the river.

I did the sketch (right) to capture the atmosphere of a still afternoon, just minutes before a heavy shower of rain, and this was achieved using pencil and watercolour. Notice how the river has very little brushwork on it, to give the illusion of stillness. As I said before, this sketch doesn't contain much detail. If I had wanted to put more detail into the bridge, I would have moved closer to it and done an information sketch in pencil.

Atmosphere sketch, *The Severn Bridge*, 2B pencil and watercolour on cartridge paper, 20 × 28 cm (8 × 11 in)

ENJOYMENT SKETCHES

My enjoyment sketch (right) was done quite spontaneously when I was in a gondola in Venice with June and my sister Shirley. There was no other reason to do the sketch than to enjoy recording the event and, although it was done very simply, it really brings back memories of that wonderful day.

June's sketch (below) of Hay Tor on Dartmoor, Devon, was done from a car park while we were waiting to meet some friends. The view inspired June, so she did a pencil sketch of it and was very happy with the result. Then, as our friends were still absent, she painted over the sketch with watercolour and thoroughly enjoyed the experience. To do a sketch just for the sheer joy of it is always very exhilarating and satisfying.

Enjoyment sketch, *Holiday in Venice*, 2B pencil on cartridge paper, 20 × 28 cm (8 × 11 in)

Enjoyment sketch, *Hay Tor, Dartmoor*, 2B pencil and watercolour on cartridge paper, 12.5 × 17 cm (5 × 7 in)

BASIC SKETCHING MATERIALS

Any medium can be used for sketching. Naturally, the less equipment you have to carry, the easier it is.

If you plan to go out for the day sketching, then you will obviously be prepared to take the equipment that is necessary for the type of work you intend to do. However, sketching is often done on the spur of the moment when the chances of having your oil painting equipment or your pastels with you are pretty remote!

One of the reasons that the pencil is such a popular sketching medium is that you can always carry one with you. A small sketchpad can also be carried in a pocket or handbag, along with a putty eraser, and with these your basic sketching kit is complete.

June has just started to use a pen more and likes this medium very much, especially for drawing people. But for general work the pencil remains the basic tool.

Everyone has a natural sketching size – mine is A4 (297 x 210 mm/11¾ x 8¼ in). You should work to the size that you are happiest with. For television, June and I often worked on an A3 (420 x 297 mm/16½ x 11¾ in) sketchpad. This was done so that the cameraman, who was filming over our shoulders, had a much larger sketching area to view.

My A4 sketchpad with 2B pencil, Black Beauty pencil and putty eraser.

USING A PENCIL

I don't need to introduce anyone to pencils. As a child, you must have used one even before you knew what it was called! But for sketching and drawing you need to know what a pencil can do and how to get the best results from it.

The pencil you buy in a shop or use in an office is called an HB pencil. This is an everyday general purpose pencil. The letters HB refer to the type of lead: H is the harder and B the softer lead. There are six hard leads and six soft ones. They are graded H, 2H, 3H, 4H, 5H and 6H (the hardest) and B, 2B, 3B, 4B, 5B and 6B (the softest) and the marks they make are illustrated on page 16. For the television series, June and I used a 2B and occasionally a 3B pencil. We also used a new pencil on the market called the Black Beauty, which is shown on my sketchpad (left) with my 2B pencil. This has a thicker lead than normal and is ideal for large, freely-drawn sketches.

To get the darkest tone from a pencil, you must put pressure on. Take the pressure off for the lightest tones. Always sharpen your pencil to a long tapering point; this enables you to use it at a flatter angle for shading. Naturally, there are many ways you can hold a pencil, but the three holds illustrated on this page are very important. The 'short hold' is the only way you can draw carefully with complete control. The 'long hold' gives you less control but more freedom with your lines. The 'flat hold' is for very free work and for shading in large areas of tone.

Now practise these different ways of using your pencil – the more you practise the better your sketches will be.

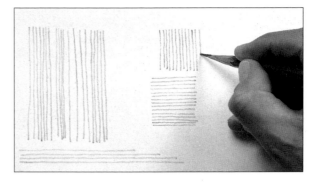

SHORT HOLD For this drawing position, hold the pencil in exactly the same way that you do for writing. This will give you complete control of your drawn lines.

LONG HOLD Hold your pencil 5–7.5 cm (2–3 in) from the point. This will allow you more freedom of movement over the paper.

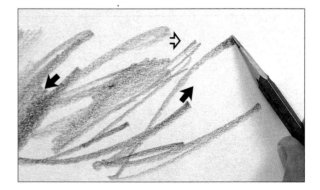

FLAT HOLD Hold the pencil almost flat on the paper, held off by your thumb and finger. This method allows you to work using the long edge of the lead for flat broad strokes and for covering large shaded areas.

THE RANGE OF PENCIL LEADS

| 6H | 5H | 4H | 3H | 2H | H | HB | B | 2B | 3B | 4B | 5B | 6B |

Short hold

Long hold

HB

2B

Black Beauty

Long hold

PRACTISE USING YOUR PENCIL

During location hunting, I couldn't decide which subject to do for an information sketch in the first television programme. I saw plenty of scenes that inspired me but they all seemed too simple, or too complicated.

I was overlooking the obvious – I love drawing and painting trees and here I was on an island full of a type of tree that I had never drawn before. Also, with nine more programmes to film, I would be very likely to need it for reference later on!

So I decided to draw a palm tree as my information sketch. When I had finished it, David, the producer, asked me to draw a couple of palm trees in the distance as a very quick enjoyment sketch and this is shown below.

While I was being filmed for television, June was busy sketching palm trees of her own!

MINUTE 3 *SKETCH*

DISTANT PALM TREES
Enjoyment sketch
2B pencil on cartridge paper, 33 × 25 cm (13 × 10 in)

Although these trees were in the distance and didn't need to be very detailed (as this was to be an enjoyment sketch done in just a few minutes), I felt much more confident having drawn the information sketch of the palm tree (opposite) a few minutes earlier. I added the sun umbrella in the foreground and also the man in the middle distance to give scale.

Doing this type of sketch isn't just enjoyable, it will also teach you to observe and simplify – two very important aspects of sketching.

PALM TREE
Information sketch
2B pencil on cartridge paper, 28 × 35 cm (11 × 14 in)

I observed this tree for ten minutes before starting to draw it and noticed two things. The first was that the trunk was reasonably smooth. I had always thought that palm tree trunks had very pronounced rings around them. This one had rings, but they were only noticeable in the different tones of the bark. The second was how much the leaves moved in the breeze. The top of the tree was changing shape all the time!

I started sketching the trunk and worked up the tree. Notice how the base of the trunk thickens and comes out of the ground at an angle. I paid particular attention to the area from which the leaves grew and drew this very carefully. I also studied the way the leaves were formed before I put them in.

SKETCHING IN WATERCOLOUR

There are many different types of watercolour boxes, brushes and colours to choose from. The equipment June and I use for all our outdoor sketching is shown on this page. I designed the Travelling Studio in 1989 as a compact sketching kit and this contains six half-pan watercolours, a water container, a sable brush and a sketching pad, 13 x 18 cm (5 x 7 in). Naturally, larger pads can be used if you prefer. It is comfortable to work standing up as the Travelling Studio has a shoulder strap and therefore rests in front of you like a tray while you work. It is lightweight, folds up and can be carried in the same way as a camera or handbag.

In addition to our six Travelling Studio colours, we also use Coeruleum. Our two main brushes are sable, but less expensive synthetic (Dalon) brushes are widely available.

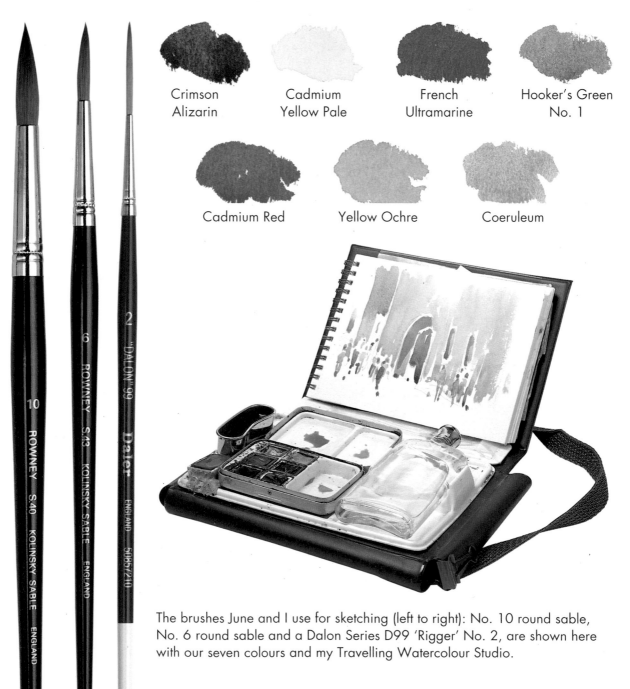

Crimson Alizarin

Cadmium Yellow Pale

French Ultramarine

Hooker's Green No. 1

Cadmium Red

Yellow Ochre

Coeruleum

The brushes June and I use for sketching (left to right): No. 10 round sable, No. 6 round sable and a Dalon Series D99 'Rigger' No. 2, are shown here with our seven colours and my Travelling Watercolour Studio.

THE FRUIT STALL, NASSAU
Information sketch
Watercolour on cartridge paper, 20 × 35 cm (8 × 14 in)

With this sketch, June experienced a few problems that can happen to us all when we work outdoors – but doesn't it make it exciting! Lorries and minibuses kept parking on the road in front of the stall and, during a heavy shower of rain, the stall holder pulled the blue plastic sheet (on the left of the sketch) over the front of the stall, hiding it completely. But June was patient and eventually finished this lively little sketch.

June drew the sketch first with a 2B pencil and then used watercolour. She wanted to capture the soft background colours, the distinctive blue plastic cover on the left, and the red and white clothes of the stall holder. Notice how the bananas are exaggerated in size. June didn't notice this until she had finished. As these were a very important visual image to show that the stall was selling fruit, June unconsciously saw them this way. Artists often exaggerate parts of a sketch – sometimes consciously, other times not – to show visually what they are trying to capture. This is good, as long as you don't overdo it.

I have already said that the three-minute sketch is one of the best ways of learning to observe and simplify. However, it isn't a test to find out who can draw the quickest!

If you find three minutes is too little time to begin with, try six or even ten minutes. But don't allow yourself too long or the object of the exercise will be lost. Pick easy subjects to start with that don't require much drawing, such as a box, a pencil or a book, and progress from these to more complicated ones.

I did the sketch of the fish on this page for television. The two sketches on the opposite page were done by June off camera, also with the timer set for three minutes.

MINUTE **3** *SKETCH*

THE THREE-MINUTE FISH
2B pencil on cartridge paper,
17 × 28 cm (7 × 11 in)

This fish had a simple shape but I drew the mouth and the eye carefully, as they were important features. I shaded the underbelly to give thickness to the body. This shading was done at an angle to show the form of the underside of the fish. I also drew a few lines on its back to show the curved shape.

These simple lines help to show that the body isn't flat. These are the kind of things that you must constantly look for and find simple ways of showing with any type of sketch.

MINUTE 3 SKETCH

MINI STRAW MARKET
2B pencil on cartridge paper, 12.5 × 17 cm (5 × 7 in)

It is quite amazing that the three stalls June sketched for this book all had distinctive shaped trees at one end. Because of this, June found the composition of each one very interesting. In the one shown here, she added a figure to give scale and life to the sketch.

TWO FIGURES
2B pencil on cartridge paper, 12.5 × 17 cm (5 × 7 in)

This young man was so flamboyant that she couldn't resist drawing him. His short, spiky hair and wide shoulders were the most important features to capture. When she had finished, June still had time to draw the back view of the policewoman on the left.

MINUTE 3 SKETCH

2

PERSPECTIVE

Don't let the word 'perspective' put you off – I know it does a lot of beginners! You do need to understand it to be able to draw correctly, but you only need to learn the basics of perspective to be able to sketch and make your work look more convincing.

Some of you will have a natural talent for perspective but, if it doesn't come naturally to you, read this chapter and, once you understand the basics, practise. By practising you will soon start to see things 'in perspective' and eventually it will become second nature.

When I am out sketching, I don't generally need to use perspective guidelines, like the ones on pages 26 to 31, because of my experience and instinct. But if my drawing looks wrong and I can't seem to get it right, I check the perspective using guidelines and this usually resolves things.

FINDING YOUR EYE LEVEL

Now let us look at the basic rules. Have you ever noticed that if you look out to sea, the horizon is always at your eye level, whether you are standing up, kneeling down or lying flat on the sand (a worm's eye view)? On television, I did this exercise on the beach which made the point very clearly. If you are in a room, you won't have a horizon, but you will still have an eye level.

To find your eye level (EL) hold a pencil horizontally in front of your eyes at arm's length. Where the pencil crosses your scene will be your eye level. A very important rule to remember is that if an object is above eye level you will be

Filming on the beach for television.

able to see underneath it, and if it is below eye level you will be able to see the top of it. The way to remind yourself about this is simple (see my illustration, above right). Take a coin and hold it horizontally in front of your eyes. You will only see the edge of the coin (a straight line) because it is on your eye level. Once you move your hand up so the coin is above your eye level, you will see underneath it. Bring the coin down below your eye level and you will see on top of it.

Try this, and then observe some other objects that are above and below your eye level.

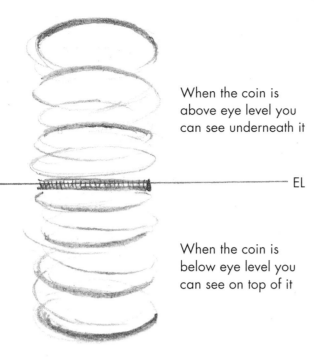

When the coin is above eye level you can see underneath it

———————————— EL

When the coin is below eye level you can see on top of it

VANISHING POINT

Now for another basic rule of perspective. All parallel lines going away from you meet at the horizon at a point which is called the vanishing point (VP). This is why railway lines appear to get closer together and finally meet in the distance (see my illustration, below centre).

On television I used the beach (see my final illustration below) to show how parallel lines meet on the eye level (horizon) at the vanishing point (VP).

Practise the exercises on pages 26 and 27 and then try some of your own. Draw boxes and simple buildings from different viewpoints. Remember to establish your eye level first, then your object in relation to it, and finally your vanishing point – the rest will follow naturally.

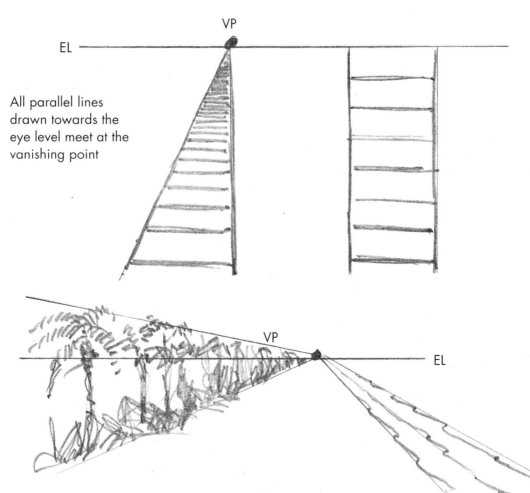

All parallel lines drawn towards the eye level meet at the vanishing point

USING BASIC PERSPECTIVE

The object of the exercise (below) is to turn a square into a cube using basic perspective. On the next page, I have taken the box a stage further to show you how to create simple buildings.

When drawing buildings from life, don't put in any detail until you have established the main structure of the building in perspective. Don't worry if you need to rub out and alter your lines. If you wish, you can use a ruler or straight edge to draw in your long perspective lines.

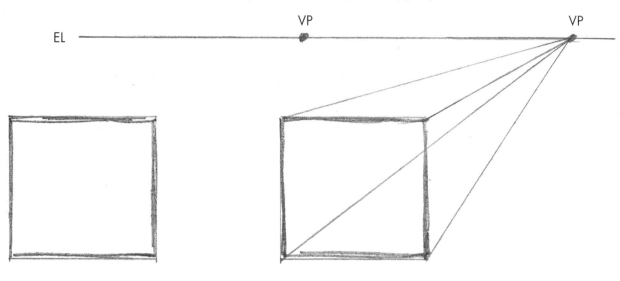

A First draw the eye level line (EL). Then draw a square below it and put a mark to the right on the eye level to use as your vanishing point (VP).

B Draw guidelines from the VP to all the corners of the square to form the top and right-hand side of the cube.

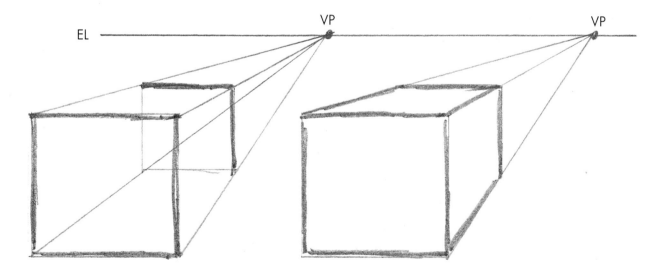

C Construct the back of the cube by connecting these guidelines with lines that are parallel to the four sides of the first square. You now have your cube and have succeeded in representing a three-dimensional object (by giving it depth) on a two-dimensional surface (your paper).

D Here the guidelines have been taken away to leave a solid box. Because this is below eye level you can see on top of the box. However, if you turn this page upside down the box will be above eye level and you will now be able to see underneath it.

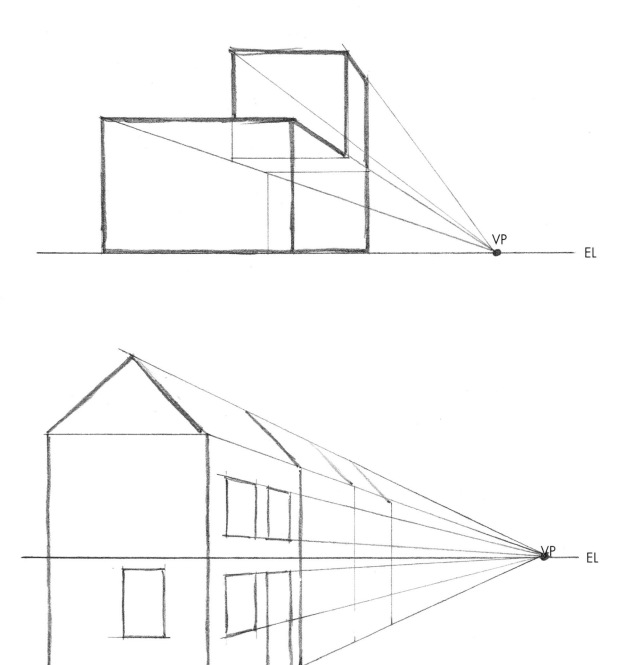

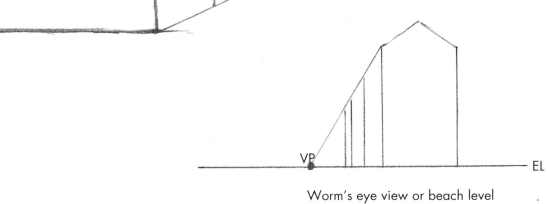

Worm's eye view or beach level

For this exercise, I wanted to find something that would show fairly simply how perspective works when you are outdoors sketching from life. When we were looking for locations, I saw the church bell outside St James' Church in Adelaide Village, New Providence Island, where June was going to be filmed sketching the congregation leaving after the service. June's sketch appears on page 74.

The bell was ideal. Notice that the canopy above it is like a box above the eye level (you can see underneath it) and you can also see inside the bell because this is above the eye level as well (remember the exercise with the coin on page 25).

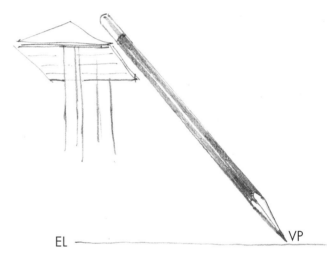

EL ————————————————— VP

THE CHURCH BELL
2B pencil on cartridge paper, 20 × 25 cm (8 × 10 in)

I started by drawing the eye level. Next I drew the roof and established the vanishing point on the eye level by holding up my pencil, with one eye closed, and positioning it against the right-hand edge of the roof. Where the pencil hit the eye level (the imaginary line that I had made with my pencil across the scene) was my vanishing point (see the illustration above). Remember that in perspective all parallel lines appear to meet at the vanishing point on the eye level. I shaded the underside of the roof darker than the top of the roof and the inside of the bell even darker. This made the bell the most important feature of the sketch.

PATRICIA'S GROCERIES
2B pencil on cartridge paper, 28 × 40 cm (11 × 16 in)

Like the church bell, this sketch was worked out by using simple perspective. The only real difference was that the building had to be divided into three sections along the front. Remember, equal 'sections' appear to get closer together as they recede into the distance. Where I started drawing the fence on the left, you can see each fence post quite distinctly but, as they get further away, the posts appear to be thinner and eventually become simplified into vertical lines joined together (see the railway line sleepers on page 25). In the same way, when drawing the three front sections, the front one was slightly wider than the middle one, and so on. When you are out sketching, distances like this can always be 'measured' to get the proportions (see page 34).

I was inspired by the colonial architecture of Patricia's Groceries, situated in a road leading up from Bay Street on Harbour Island. I only did this in pencil but it was very paintable. It was also an oasis for us and we gave it full marks for its ice-cold orange juice! This sketch wasn't shown on television but I have included it here because it is a good subject to demonstrate perspective.

You will notice that I sketched it quite simply. When drawing, it is important to remember that you are not trying to be an architect, otherwise you will lose the lovely freedom that comes with sketching. Use perspective 'lines' as guides only.

A few minutes of relaxation – for me, if not for June!

After June had suggested to David that she should sketch me relaxing in the hammock as a three-minute sketch for television, she said to me just before filming: 'I think I might have been a little over-confident with this one!'

But the hammock had inspired June and, although it probably wasn't the easiest of subjects to choose to do under pressure, being inspired is the most important part of deciding what to sketch.

ALWYN IN A HAMMOCK
Black Beauty pencil on cartridge paper,
28 × 40 cm (11 × 16 in)

June decided the placing of my head was the most important part of the drawing and so she spent time getting the correct position for it. Although the hammock strings were not important for general detail, the overall shape they formed was, since this would lend movement to the hammock. My leg and foot were drawn carefully, which helped to establish my relaxed pose. June's most important objective in the three minutes was to get the impression of me looking completely at ease. I certainly enjoyed my part in it – and liked the sketch, too!

MINUTE **3** *SKETCH*

3

MEASURING

Two of the most difficult aspects of sketching and drawing for the beginner are getting objects in proportion to one another and fitting a drawing onto a sketchpad without running out of paper! The way to tackle both problems is to learn how to measure your scene and to transfer those measurements to your paper. This is one of the most important lessons you will learn in this course and, taken step by step, it's not as difficult as it sounds.

I introduced this programme from Coral Sands Beach on Harbour Island. From where I stood I could see a bandstand with a palm tree next to it but I had no real idea of the size of either the stand or the tree until June walked into the picture. This immediately gave scale since I could relate her to the rest of the scene.

I then demonstrated how to get the whole of that scene onto my sketchpad with everything in proportion by using my pencil to measure the scene.

USING A KEY MEASURE

First I measured June with my pencil to give me a 'key measure', which I would use throughout the drawing. Next I held my pencil vertically in front of the scene and found that my key measure went into the whole scene (from the bottom of the bandstand to the top of the tree) about five times. At this point, I had to guess the height June would need to be in my drawing in order to fit everything else into my sketch. On television, I put two marks on my pad to represent her but this first key measure was too big since I could only get three 'Junes' onto the

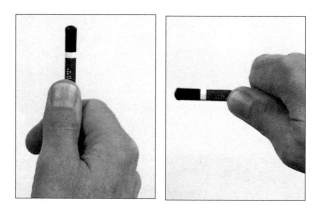

Hold your pencil at arm's length, vertically for vertical measurements and horizontally for horizontal measurements, using your thumb as a marker.

In this drawing, I used June as my key measure.

page. I then made her smaller and got five 'Junes' in. This meant that I could get all the picture onto the page. The simple drawing I did of June, the bandstand and the palm tree is shown (below left).

In the photograph, below, I used the house in the middle of the picture as my key measure. There is no rule to say what you should use but it should be a convenient size to work with.

You will see that I measured parts of the scene both horizontally and vertically to work out sizes and proportions using key measures and half key measures. Naturally, before drawing the scene on my sketchpad, I had to decide what size my key measure should be but, once this was established, I knew I could fit the whole of the scene onto my paper. Incidentally, if I wanted to draw this scene on a very small or very large piece of paper, I would measure it in

exactly the same way. The size you make your key measure determines scale and enables you to fit a scene onto the paper.

In this case, I saw that my key measure needed to go across my sketchpad ten times horizontally and seven times vertically in order for the whole scene to fit onto my sketchpad. So, if I had made the key measure 5 cm (2 in) long, my paper would have had to be 50 cm (20 in) wide, and so on.

Try some measuring now from wherever you are sitting – it works exactly the same way indoors and outdoors. In time, with practice, your eyes will become aware of scale and proportion and you will only refer to 'measuring' when you can't work something out, or when something looks wrong. This will happen! However, I rarely do a detailed sketch from life without checking and measuring something.

Use your key measure to get the correct proportions in a scene.

USING COLOURED PENCILS

I am sure we have all used coloured pencils at some stage in our lives, especially when we were young. Our parents gave them to us simply because they were easy to use and weren't messy.

Years ago, the lead in coloured pencils tended to be rather hard and, although they were ideal for general colour work, I didn't find them satisfactory for sketching. However, while I have been busy working with other mediums, coloured pencils have advanced tremendously and they are now an exciting medium to use.

The ones that June and I used for television were the Derwent Artists Pencils (shown right). They are soft and blend easily (see below) to create an infinite range of colours.

THE SHELL DOME
Coloured pencils on cartridge paper,
28 × 35 cm (11 × 14 in)

When you go out with your sketchpad, try not to have preconceived ideas about what you are going to sketch (see Programme 4: Choosing A Subject).

When we were looking for subjects on Paradise Island, which is reached by bridge from New Providence Island, June was inspired by the Shell Dome at the Atlantis Hotel and decided to draw it for this programme.

Unfortunately, for practical reasons, we couldn't film her doing this until the late afternoon. By that time the position of the sun had, of course, changed and the scene wasn't nearly as inspiring.

Also, June had to sketch the building from a completely different angle to the one we had first seen it from. In fact, her sketching position for television was at the edge of the water with sharks and stingrays swimming around – but she still coped admirably!

The building was established first without detail. The proportions of the dome with the shell on top and the building underneath it were the important elements to be measured. The right-hand side of the dome was left pale, without a dark outline, and this helped to give the impression of the dome being round. June's suggestion of palm trees and figures in the sketch was very important to give scale to the building.

I chose this view from Parliament Square in Nassau because the red door was easy to see and made a good key measure. The palm trees in front of the buildings also helped me to draw in key elements since they were like ready-made markers positioned across the scene. I only put two people into the sketch and didn't worry about passing cars or carriages because I wanted to show the principle of measuring and didn't want to confuse the exercise.

There is one very important point to remember when you are working from nature. Don't worry about being too exact when measuring either from the scene or onto your paper. 'Nearly half a measure', 'a measure and a bit' or 'just under a full measure' is accurate enough. If you try to fit everything exactly to a full key measure you will get very frustrated and your measuring will become a hindrance to your sketching, not an aid.

PARLIAMENT SQUARE, NASSAU
2B pencil and coloured pencils on cartridge paper,
28 × 40 cm (11 × 16 in)

After finding and deciding the key measure, I made sure that I could fit the scene onto my pad. I started by measuring the two buildings and drawing them in outline. I then measured and positioned the windows. Incidentally, I made the windows too wide to start with so I rubbed them out and started again. It happens to us all! Remember that an eraser is as much a part of your equipment as a pencil. Finally, when I was happy with the building, I drew in the palm trees.

This time it was my turn for a three-minute sketch! This garden chair with its tubular frame looks complicated and was quite a challenge to do in so short a time. But if you can imagine the chair as a box, like the one you did in the perspective programme, then you can understand the shape of it much better (see the example, right). Naturally, some of the angles of the chair are not perpendicular or horizontal like a box, but the basic shape and the principle of drawing is the same.

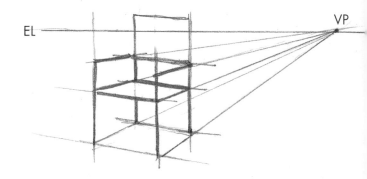

MINUTE 3 SKETCH

GARDEN CHAIR
2B pencil on cartridge paper, 20 × 15 cm (8 × 6 in)

After quickly measuring and checking the proportions, the most important shape to establish was the seat of the chair, so I drew this first. The four legs and back were then positioned. I added detail and strength to the drawing with the time I had left.

SKETCHING WITH CHARCOAL

You very rarely see artists using charcoal. Perhaps this is because it is a messy medium – it smudges easily and you get very dirty hands! However, it is well worth coming to terms with these problems and having a go.

Charcoal is extremely versatile and you can capture atmosphere and form in simple, quick strokes. This makes it ideal for fast sketching. You can smudge it with your finger to get subtle grey tones and rub it out with a putty eraser. This is another medium I suggest you definitely try. You will need to fix your charcoal sketches to stop them smudging when you have finished (see page 94).

I was introduced to charcoal at art school but have hardly used it since then. So, when June and I decided to use it in the television series, it was like discovering a new medium.

To sketch a subject like this, as June did in just three minutes, you have to do your measuring by eye. In this case, there wasn't time to do anything else, particularly with the people in the band moving around and with holidaymakers walking in front of the scene and blocking it out at times. But when you have practised measuring, you will find that gradually you are able to judge things by eye. Even so, this was quite a challenge for June. Lots of people had gathered around and many were standing behind the cameras watching her work. The calypso music was very loud and exciting, the sun was hot and the whole area seemed to be throbbing to the beat of the Caribbean music.

In fact, June's charcoal was moving very fast over the page all the time. From where I was watching, trying to keep people from walking in front of the cameras, I was sure that the charcoal and June were moving to the music!

MINUTE 3 *SKETCH*

THE BAND
Charcoal on cartridge paper, 28 × 40 cm (11 × 16 in)

June drew the musicians first. The man on the left was important because he was in full view and the easiest figure to recognize. The bandstand and the pillars were then drawn in, and this gave stability to the sketch.

Finally, a simple line was sketched in to suggest the rocks in front of the bandstand. June didn't use any smudging techniques in this sketch – there simply wasn't time.

4

CHOOSING A SUBJECT

If you see something that inspires you to sketch, you have found your subject. But it doesn't always work as easily as that because we think there may be something better around the next corner and off we go in search of Utopia!

This is the biggest danger when you sketch outdoors. I have had the occasional day when I have kept looking for something 'better' to sketch and finished up doing nothing and being very cross and frustrated at the end of the day. Try not to go out with preconceived ideas of what you want to sketch, because that subject or scene may not be there. Have an open mind and be prepared to sketch and enjoy what is available. But as soon as you see something that excites you, stop and sketch it. It is important to remember that, if you are inspired by a scene, you will produce your best work. If there is something better round the next corner, you can do that next!

I designed this picture finder to help beginners.

FINDING YOUR PICTURE

If you are looking at a panoramic landscape or a village street, you may have problems deciding which part of the scene to draw, or where to start or finish your sketch. To help yourself, cut out a rectangle in a piece of card approximately 5 x 7.5 cm (2 x 3 in). Hold this makeshift viewfinder up in front of your scene, close one eye and move it around. The closer you have it to your eye, the more you will see of the scene; the further away it is, the less you will see of it. Move it around until you find the exact scene you want to paint.

Every sketch should have a centre of interest or focal point. This is the important part of the sketch that we want the viewer to see first and also keeps the eye from wandering all over the picture not knowing where to stop. Although it can be anything you choose, there is a simple and traditional rule about placing your centre of interest on your paper.

If you divide your paper into thirds across and down, any of the four points at which the lines cross is accepted as a happy position on the painting. On television I used the picture finder (below left) which I designed a few years ago to help beginners. The 'window' is covered by acetate and is divided into thirds with black lines. This enables you to position your centre of interest as you look at your scene through it. The simple sketches (right) are the ones I drew for television to show where to put the focal point or centre of interest in a picture.

The first sketch shows the church clock as the centre of interest, while the second one uses the church door as its focal point. Naturally, parts of your picture will fall at the four points where the centre of interest could go but it is the part of the painting that you wish to show most prominently that you should concentrate on and make your focal point. The final sketch has a group of people with their heads placed at the centre of interest.

I must stress that, although traditionally accepted, this is only a rule of thumb in design and you shouldn't let it restrict you too much. Keep experimenting and being creative!

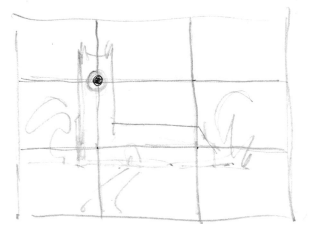

In this sketch, the clock on the church steeple provides the focal point.

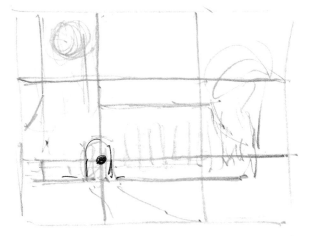

The door of the church is the centre of interest in this sketch.

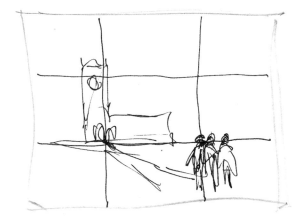

The three people in this sketch have been placed so that their heads are in a centre of interest position.

USING OIL COLOURS

On television, I used an easel when painting in oils to make it easier for the cameras, but normally I would have used my Oil Travelling Studio (pictured below).

This is a wooden pochade box that holds everything that you need and rests on your knees when you work. The lid acts as an easel and holds a 15 x 20 cm (6 x 8 in) size board to work on. You can purchase a larger one that takes a 25 x 30 cm (10 x 12 in) size board and I also use this for sketching.

The best quality oil paints are called Artists' Professional quality and the grade below them are students' colours. I normally use Georgian Oil Colours, a students' quality, and my colours are shown on the next page.

I only used the three brushes shown below for the painting on page 49. These are (from left to right) a Daler-Rowney sable Series 43 No. 6 and

Bristlewhite Series B.48 Nos. 2 and 4. I used Low Odour Thinners (turpentine substitute) and Alkyd Flow Medium, which I added to the paints as I worked in order to speed up the drying time.

Surfaces (grounds) for working in oil colours are numerous. You can use canvas, primed hardboard, primed watercolour paper, ready-made oil painting boards, ready-primed oil sketching paper (which comes in sheets or pads) and Cryla paper which is made especially for acrylic and oil painting.

Naturally, as with all materials, the choice is yours. However, if you are a beginner, I suggest you start with the basic materials and let your own experience guide you around your local art suppliers later on.

I really enjoy using oils for sketching. Although you can't work as much detail into a sketch with them as you can with pencil, watercolour or acrylics, you can paint the

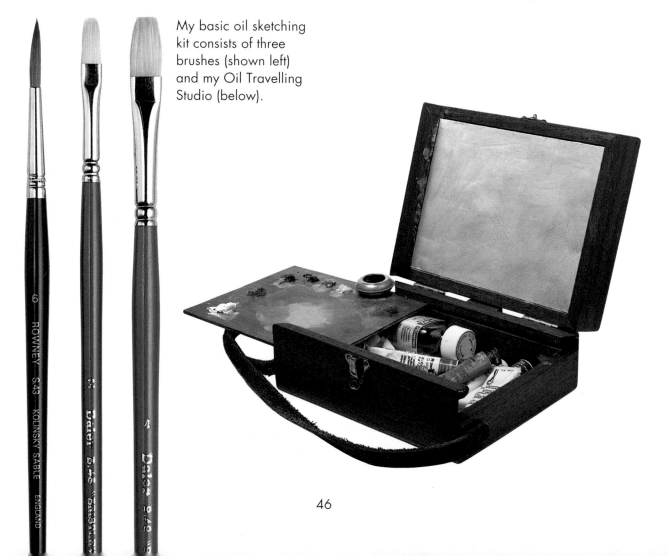

My basic oil sketching kit consists of three brushes (shown left) and my Oil Travelling Studio (below).

| Crimson Alizarin | Cadmium Yellow | Cobalt Blue | Viridian |

| Coeruleum | Cadmium Red | Raw Umber | Yellow Ochre |

I used the eight colours above (plus white) when sketching in oils for television.

impression of a scene quickly with oils and can also wipe out passages and start again if you find you want to change them – something that isn't very easy to do when working with watercolour and is almost impossible with acrylics.

Incidentally, working in oil doesn't mean you have to paint large sketches – don't forget that you can work small, like my sketch (right) of a white and blue boat that we saw one day in the tranquil setting of Harbour Island.

A peaceful mooring, Harbour Island.
Oil on primed hardboard with a Raw Sienna wash, 20 × 10 cm (8 × 4 in)

I was really inspired by the lovely harbour when we first got off the boat at Harbour Island and could have sat and painted it there and then. However, it was a few days before I actually got the chance to sketch it for television. There were several exciting aspects to choose from but, using my picture finder, I decided to make the sunlit building on the right of the picture my focal point when I sketched it for television.

The object of this exercise was to do an atmosphere sketch. I wanted to capture the bright colours, especially the light turquoise of the sea and the warmth of this Caribbean island. When you create a sketch like this, you really get a feeling of the place.

If I had wanted more detail in order to help me work on a painting from my sketch back at home, I would have done a pencil information sketch and taken photographs of the scene to aid my memory.

VIEW AT HARBOUR ISLAND
Oil on Cryla paper painted with a wash of Raw Sienna, 25 × 30 cm (10 × 12 in)

I drew the picture with my No. 6 sable brush using a thin turpsy colour mixed from Cobalt Blue and Crimson Alizarin. I continued by filling in the trees and dark areas very freely (see the halfway stage, below).

Although the sketch wasn't detailed, I had to paint some areas carefully to keep their shape and form. These were the white roofs, the right-hand shed, the boats and the figures.

Notice how I didn't paint over the sky but left this as the original Raw Sienna background as this helped to unify the painting. The strong contrast between the bright and dark colours gives the scene a sunny look.

Above all, when doing this sketch, I tried hard not to fiddle!

Halfway stage

48

Finished stage

Painting the scene for television.

The blue shutters on this white colonial-style
house inspired June to paint this sketch
although they were only a very small part of the
scene she was looking at. Notice how she put
them in a good centre-of-interest position in the
painting. June was using a sketchbook that
didn't have 'ring binding'. This makes it easier
to work onto the left-hand page if you want to
expand your sketch. She did this, and added
more sky and sea.

HOUSE WITH BLUE SHUTTERS
Watercolour on cartridge paper,
25 × 35 cm (10 × 14 in)

June left the white house as unpainted paper. The
windows and shutters were important so she
painted them carefully. The picket fence was
formed by painting the background between the
fence posts, leaving them as white paper. June was
careful not to paint the palm leaves over the white
house (although, in the real scene, they were
blowing over it most of the time). She felt the
turquoise sea was also very important, although
she used a simple brush stroke to suggest it.

Conch fish seems to be the staple diet for many of the Bahamian people. It is prepared for eating in many different ways, such as conch salad, conch chowder, conch fritters and even conch burgers!

June decided the moment she first saw a conch shell that she would like to sketch one. Their lovely deep red and pale pink colours really inspired her. Little did she know that, when she did draw one for television, it would be a three-minute sketch – and in charcoal!

MINUTE 3 *SKETCH*

CONCH SHELL
Charcoal on cartridge paper, 15 × 17 cm (6 × 7 in)

The most important thing to establish in this drawing was the darkest dark and the lightest light. June did this by screwing her eyes up to look at the object (see Programme 5: Tonal Values). The middle tones were made by taking the pressure off the charcoal, or simply smudging it with the finger. The lightest areas were left as white paper and the very dark areas were achieved by putting pressure on the charcoal.

SWAYING PALM TREES
2B pencil on cartridge paper, 25 × 20 cm (10 × 8 in)

There was a very violent thunderstorm one night while we were staying on Harbour Island and, when we got up early the following morning, the dawn sky was still full of angry windswept clouds.

June looked at the swaying palm trees with their branches blowing wildly about in the wind and felt incredibly inspired. She didn't have to search for her subject that day! However, she still had to decide which part of the scene in front of her to make into a picture, and one which would be both an atmosphere and an enjoyment sketch.

June used the 'long hold' for her pencil (see page 15) to give her freedom with her lines. Although there is a tremendous amount of movement in the sketch, the eye seems to settle on the left-hand palm tree, where the coconuts grow. The centre of interest in this sketch is in the same position as the church clock in my first example on page 45.

5

TONAL VALUES

We all need to understand tonal values because they help us to create form and shape. All four boxes on page 55 were drawn in the same way – it is the tonal values that change their appearance. My pencil drawings are in black and white but, naturally, if you were sketching from life the tones you would be looking at would be in colour.

The best way to find the tonal values in a scene is to screw your eyes up. You will then see that the dark and light areas stand out clearly and mid-tones and detail disappear. When you sketch, look at colours in this way to see them in relation to the whole of the picture. Ask yourself, 'How light or how dark is the blue compared to the light and dark of the yellow?' and so on. Take time to look at the scene, then look and find (with your eyes screwed up) the darkest and lightest areas.

Keep practising and you will soon begin to see your subjects in terms of their tonal values.

If you look at fig. **A** on the opposite page, you will see that this shaded area without any light source has no form and just looks like a flat silhouette. However, once we add a light source, see fig. **B**, this light hits the object and creates tonal areas which show its form as a box.

If we look at this simply, the shape of the box is made clear to us by dark areas against light areas. Even the top of the box at its two furthest edges is formed only by pencil lines but these show dark against the white background.

In fig. **C**, the light source is coming from the right and this changes the tonal values on the sides of the box. The light is stronger on the top than it is on the right-hand side and the darkest area is on the front of the box where there is very little light and it is in shadow.

Now look at fig. **D**. The light is coming from the left again but you can see how, by using light and shade (dark against light), I have made this box appear to be without a lid.

Here June was sketching the blue fruit stall, shown on page 66.

light source

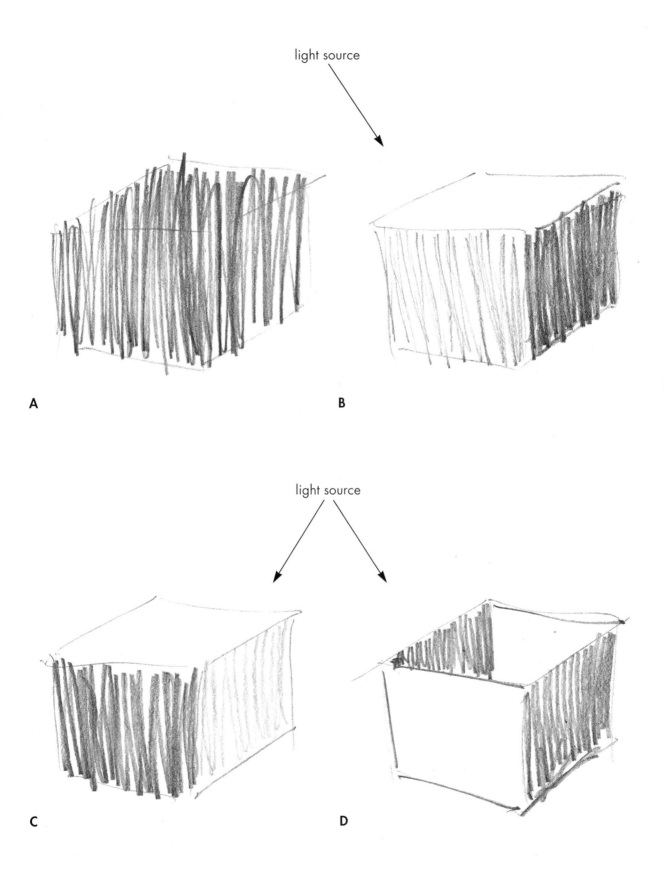

A

B

light source

C

D

The boxes from **A** to **E** are the same shape as the boxes on the previous page. Look at each one carefully and see how, by using dark and light tones, the form of the box has changed. In **A** it has become a 'sleeve', while **B** could be either the same box turned around, or a box on its side without a lid. In **C** the inside of the box has been partitioned to make one part of it solid. Box **D** is a box with its lid open and box **E** is an aquarium. So although the same outline was drawn for all these boxes, they were made to look different by tonal shading.

In fig. **F**, I have drawn several boxes of different sizes together. Look at the ringed areas where two equal tones merge together. The corner of the box is lost where the dark is against dark and appears again where the dark goes against light. This is called 'lost and found'.

In real life, shapes are lost to the eye when their tonal values are equal. This helps to make a painting look more realistic so let it happen in your sketches, unless you want that particular area to read (to show its shape or form).

Fig. **G** is the same as **F**, except that the light source is coming from the opposite direction.

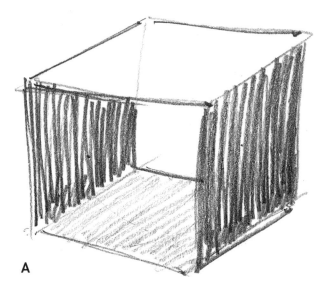

A

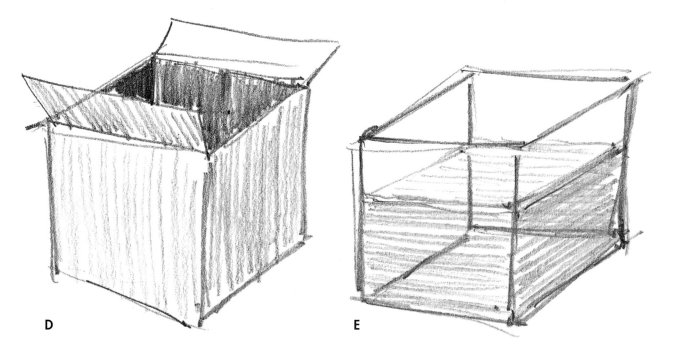

D

E

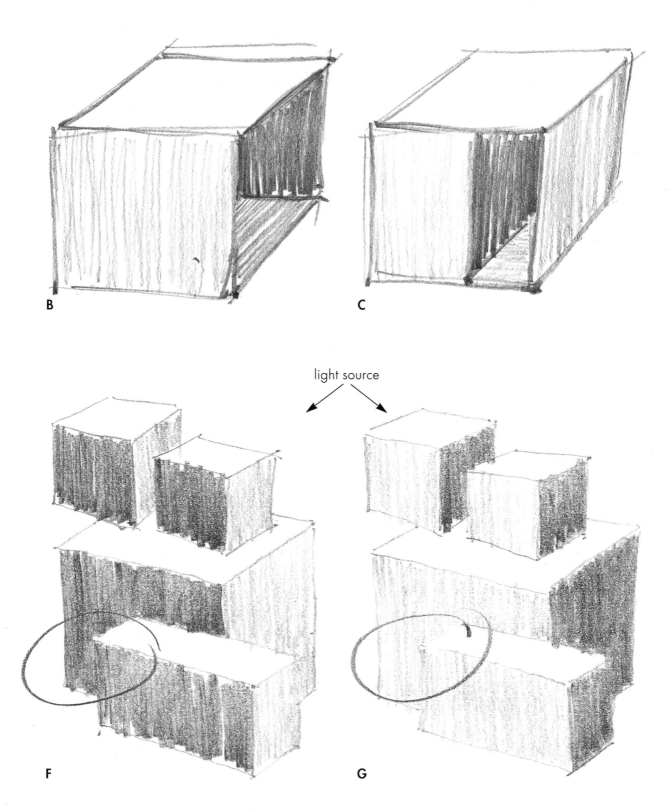

B

C

light source

F

G

One of the best ways of learning to see tonal values is to work in black and white. For television, I decided to draw a bowl of fruit to demonstrate this, as it would give me some definite shapes to work to.

So far I have been showing you how square shapes are formed by tonal areas. With the fruit in this picture, most of the shapes are oval or round. This means that the dark areas gradually merge into lighter areas without a definite sharp edge.

BOWL OF FRUIT
Charcoal on cartridge paper, 28 × 35 cm (11 × 14 in)

I did the drawing first with a 2B pencil, then looked very carefully to see the tonal values of the fruit and, in particular, their light and dark sides. As the light is coming from the right, the darker side of each fruit is on the left. However, notice how shadows cast by some fruit can fall on the light side of other fruit. Because of this, you can have a dark side on a light side – see the apple.

I used my finger to soften the edges of the shading and to merge dark into light. You can also soften edges and take out charcoal with a putty eraser.

USING ACRYLIC COLOURS

For television, I used my Acrylic Travelling Studio (shown below). Like the Oil Travelling version (on page 46), it carries all you need and takes a 15 x 20 cm (6 x 8 in) painting board to work on. However, for my sketch of the Grouper fish on page 64, I used a 25 x 30 cm (10 x 12 in) piece of Cryla paper fastened onto a board, which rested against the lid.

I use Daler-Rowney Artists' Cryla Flow Colours for all my acrylic work. For television, I used the eight colours shown on the next page. In addition to these, I also used white.

As acrylic paint is water-based, the only medium I used to mix with them was water. Never let the paint dry in your brush and always make sure you wash your brushes out in water when you have finished with them.

There are brushes made specially for use with acrylics and the ones I normally use are Cryla Series C25. For the painting in this programme I used a No. 8 brush from this series, together with my No. 6 sable brush (shown opposite).

There are many surfaces which you can use for acrylic work. Apart from Cryla paper, you can work on any watercolour paper, primed hardboard, ready-made boards, canvas and even brown wrapping paper.

Finally, I recommend you use a Daler-Rowney Stay-Wet Palette. If you follow the instructions, this will keep your paints wet and usable on your palette almost indefinitely. It will also save you a lot of paint!

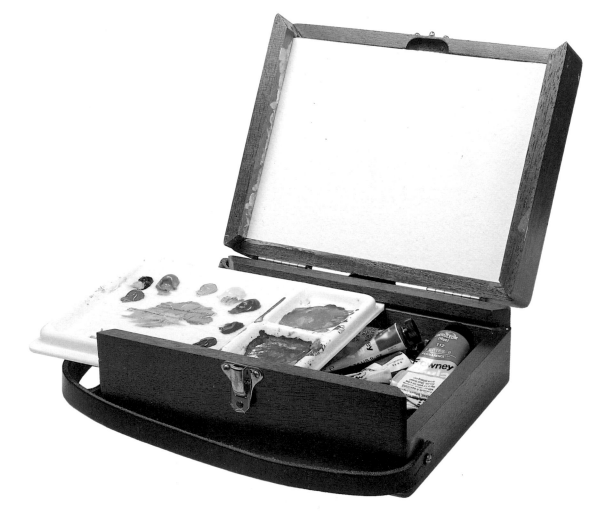

My Acrylic Travelling Studio.

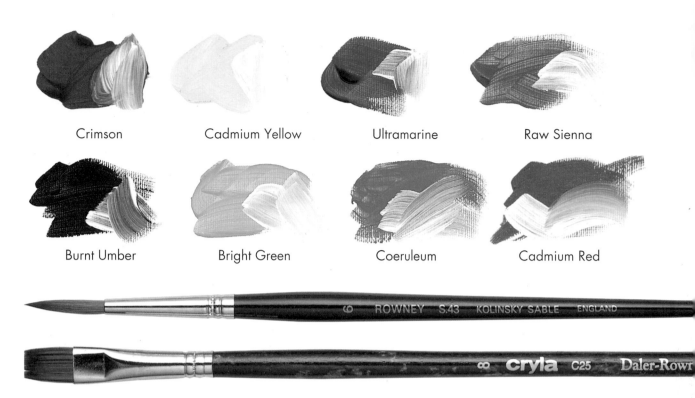

Crimson	Cadmium Yellow	Ultramarine	Raw Sienna
Burnt Umber	Bright Green	Coeruleum	Cadmium Red

I used eight colours (plus white) and just two brushes when sketching in acrylics for television.

Small acrylic sketches, like my example (right), are great fun to paint. The only danger is that you can overwork them, since acrylic paint dries quickly and gives you the opportunity to keep overpainting and fiddling! I always tell myself not to do this because I think it spoils the spontaneity of a picture. But, of course, this is up to the individual artist. If you like putting a lot of work into your sketches, then by all means do so – there are no set rules!

A small market in Nassau. Acrylic on Cryla paper, 25 × 17 cm (10 × 7 in)

My painting set-up.

We bought this fish from one of the local fishermen and I decided that it would be a perfect subject to sketch using my acrylic colours. I have done the pencil drawing (below) to give you an idea of what I saw when I screwed up my eyes to see the tonal values. Remember that you will always see exaggerated light and dark areas. Practise looking at objects like this to get used to seeing colours as tones of dark and light.

THE GROUPER FISH
Acrylic on Cryla paper with a Raw Sienna and Crimson wash, 25 × 30 cm (10 × 12 in)

First stage
I drew the fish with a 2B pencil first. I didn't draw in any detail but the overall shape was important. The large head and big lips of this fish are distinctive and I took care with this part of the drawing. (Always look for special characteristics when you start any drawing and make sure you capture them.) I didn't intend to paint the dish but drew in its shape to help me with the positioning of the fish.

Halfway stage
I started painting from head to tail using a watery mix of Burnt Umber. I added a little Ultramarine for darker areas and a touch of Bright Green in places. The pink areas were mixed from Cadmium Red, Cadmium Yellow and Crimson and on these I used the paint in the same way as watercolour. I used it thicker (not as watery) further down the body, and added white to suggest the shiny surface of the fish.

▲ *First stage*

▼ *Halfway stage*

Finished stage

I concentrated on the head next, making the paint darker and adding more form and shape. I used thicker paint and added more white into the mixes. Throughout the painting, I worked the brush strokes in the direction of the shape of the body because this helped to show form. I also let the background colour show through by painting thinly in places, which helped to unify the painting.

I left the eye until last. I felt that if the fish looked good without the eye, it would look even better once this was painted. This is just one of my artistic quirks. I always like to leave something until last to be the 'icing on the cake' and then finish my painting with it. Aren't we artists a funny lot!

June decided to sketch this quaint little fruit and vegetable stall for television as it was ideal for demonstrating tonal work. It was also very attractively situated on the side of the harbour, just waiting to be painted!

June didn't bother to put in the background or the passers-by, because she didn't want to complicate the exercise.

If you look at her pencil illustrations (below) you will see that, in its simplest form and without a light source, the stall would be a silhouette like the first box on page 55.

With a light source added (the sun, in this case) the front is in shadow and the right-hand side is the lightest side.

THE BLUE FRUIT STALL
Watercolour on cartridge paper,
28 × 40 cm (11 × 16 in)

Jun'e used three 'blue' tones to give the stall a three-dimensional look. The lightest tone of blue, a mixture of Coeruleum and French Ultramarine, was painted on the front and the side of the stall first (as in the pencil silhouette, left). When this was dry, the front of the stall (the shadow side) was painted with a darker blue wash.

The inside of the stall, seen through the doorway, was the darkest tone of all. Notice how this gives depth to the stall. June didn't paint the fruit and vegetables too brightly, as they were in shadow, and the white doors on the front of the stall were painted over with a warm grey wash to keep these in shadow, too.

6

MOVING OBJECTS

It isn't easy to draw moving objects and, unfortunately, there are many subjects – people, animals, birds, vehicles, even clouds – that will not keep still for the artist. This means we have to train ourselves to be able to sketch them and the basic recipe for success is practice!

The sketching formula I use is this. Watch your subject and study it carefully before you start to draw. How long you do this for is up to you – it could be five minutes or half an hour. Having looked at your subject, keep the image in your mind's eye and start drawing. Then look at it again, taking in as much visual reference as you can hold at one time, and return to your drawing. Repeat this until the object moves out of your view.

STOP AND START AGAIN

Depending on the speed or movement of your subject, you may be able to keep working for a few minutes. If you are sketching a horse and it moves to another position just when you have started, you will need to stop and start again with the new position. If you are part-way through and you have to stop, leave that sketch unfinished and start another one. Nine times out of ten, the horse will resume the first position and then you can carry on with the previous sketch. Or you may see another horse in that particular position and be able to use that one for reference to complete your sketch.

Often when I have been out drawing cows in a field, one sketch will be made up from three animals. I'll use the head of one, the legs of another, and so on. Apart from enjoying

I couldn't finish the drawing of the guard on the right because he changed position. But I could paint in the colours as the guards were still on parade.

the experience of sketching moving objects, you are always gathering information. The more knowledge you accumulate about a particular subject, the easier it will be for you next time you have the opportunity to sketch it.

At first your sketches may not be that good. You will find it can take up to fifteen minutes before your pencil and brain work together at speed and your drawings start to look like the animal you are sketching. June and I find this happens to us on many occasions.

SKETCHING PEOPLE

Three-minute sketches can be a tremendous learning aid for sketching moving objects because, as I have said before, this discipline teaches you to observe, simplify and work fast.

Sketching the changing of the guard, which takes place in front of the Governor's House in Nassau every two weeks, was a real challenge. We didn't know how the ceremony would be performed and I could only guess which would be my best sketching position. Also, we only had one chance to film this as we wouldn't be in Nassau for the next ceremony.

Luck was on our side and the only problem was tourists obscuring my view as I painted. This is a hazard that you can never completely eliminate – even with cameras around you and a very helpful policeman standing nearby who had been detailed to help us out.

THE CHANGING OF THE GUARD
2B pencil and watercolour on cartridge paper,
25 × 38 cm (10 × 15 in)

This sketch is of part of the Royal Bahamas Police Band. I didn't have time to draw any more of them before they moved off again, although they came back a little later on and I was able to add some colour. Notice how the dark green background helps to show the shape of the guards' white jackets (light against dark). With this type of subject, I always do the drawing first. When this is finished and I am happy with it, I add colour if there is time.

THE BAND PLAYED ON
2B pencil on cartridge paper, 25 × 38 cm (10 × 15 in)

The sketch (above left) is of the band coming towards me as they marched by. Having less than half a minute to sketch them really did get my pencil working fast and my adrenalin flowing! I had a little more time to do the other figures (shown above and left).

Always try to retain as much of the image of a scene as possible in your mind's eye while you draw it. If you want to use sketches like these to work from later, you will need to take some photographs to help you and also make colour notes. These, with your memory of the scene and the knowledge gained while sketching it, will provide you with enough information to paint a picture back home.

USING PENS

With so many pens on the market, which one should you choose? The thickness of the nib, and therefore the line it creates, is very much a matter of personal preference, as is the general design of the pen. Always look for a pen that feels well-balanced and is comfortable to draw with. Also make sure that it is waterproof so that, should you decide to turn your drawing into a pen and wash (see page 77), you will be able to paint over your pen marks without any fear of them running.

June and I used black Uni Pin Fine Line markers, which were waterproof and fadeproof, for our pen drawings on television. We also used Uni-Ball Signo pens and our coloured felt-tip pens with a 'brush-like' nib were Lyra Aquabrushes. Finally, I used a biro for my sketch on page 89.

While I was being filmed, June was also busy doing these sketches of the guards and some people in the crowd. She used her felt-tip pens to add colour to some of her pen drawings.

Below (left to right): Lyra Aquabrushes in Red and Black, Uni-Ball Signo and Uni Pin Fine Line Marker

For days, June had been looking forward to sketching the congregation leaving St James' Church in Adelaide Village. She had imagined groups of people, some in flamboyant hats, standing around and chatting to one another outside the church door.

However, when the door opened at the end of the service, most of the people rushed away – perhaps to their Sunday lunch! So, unfortunately for June, a crowd didn't materialize and her pencil and watercolour sketch is of individuals rather than a big group – and there were no hats! As I said earlier, always be prepared for your subject matter to change.

LEAVING CHURCH
2B pencil and watercolour on cartridge paper,
17 × 25 cm (7 × 10 in)

June drew Father Brown in the doorway first, as he was the important figure, with his white robe against the dark doorway. When he was established, the other figures were drawn as they came out of the church. June painted them with watercolours after the pencil drawing was complete. Notice the railings on the right. Since, unlike the people, these didn't move, June had time to paint them in more carefully, although she did them as freely as the people. If the railings had been done too neatly they would not look part of the sketch. The two pencil drawings of groups of people (right) were done after the filming.

Before doing this three-minute sketch, I thought that the policeman, standing in one position, would be much easier to draw than the guards had been. However, the working conditions were fairly difficult.

I was sitting on a stone step on the pavement which wasn't very comfortable, and traffic kept stopping in front of the policeman while I did the sketch. It had never obscured him from view before I started! But there's never a dull moment when you sketch outside and this is why it is so exciting – it really makes you aware of life around you, whether you are in a town or in the countryside.

THE TRAFFIC POLICEMAN
2B pencil on cartridge paper,
25 × 15 cm (10 × 6 in)

I drew the policeman first, starting with his head and working down to his feet.

Notice how you can see on top of the box he is standing on. This is because it was below my eye level. You can see underneath the umbrella because this was above my eye level.

If this had been a 'normal time' sketch, I would have suggested some of the surroundings to show that the policeman was situated in the middle of the road.

MINUTE **3** SKETCH

FLAMINGOS
2B pencil, watercolour and felt pen on cartridge paper,
25 × 30 cm (10 × 12 in)

Before drawing them, June carefully studied the flamingos. The important features to observe were the strangely-shaped beak, the long thin neck and the very long thin legs.

Remember, when your model moves, go onto another one. June painted the flamingos with watercolour after the drawings had been done. She used felt-tip pens for the last one. Afterwards, she felt the colour was too strong, and wished she had used a paler felt-tip pen.

By the time the television crew were ready to film June sketching them, these flamingos were a little uneasy about the cameras. This made them hold their long necks very straight, which took away some of their lovely flowing curves.

7

PEN & WASH TECHNIQUES

With pen and wash, you draw your sketch with a 'dip-in' pen and waterproof Indian ink, a waterproof drawing pen, or a fine-line marker like the one shown on page 72. Then you paint over your sketch with watercolour paints. Or you can reverse this method and paint with watercolour first, then draw over the painting with pen. It is entirely up to you which of these techniques you use.

We did the whole of this television programme in the Straw Market in Nassau, a bustling area of small stalls where you can buy almost anything made from straw. It was a very colourful and lively scene and made a good subject for pen and wash.

A CORNER OF THE STRAW MARKET
Pen and watercolour wash on cartridge paper,
28 × 33 cm (11 × 13 in)

I drew the scene first in pencil. Then I painted watercolour freely over the whole of the drawing. The darker shadow areas and the dark interior were painted over when this was dry.

Next I used my fine-line marker freely and without fussy detail to give the impression of loosely-stacked straw products, although I drew the shapes of the hats and bags carefully.

Notice how freely I drew the leaves. I painted the shadows of the tree on the ground last. After debating whether to put these in, I finally decided to do it, as it would help to suggest sunlight. I like this sketch but think perhaps I should have made the inside of the doorway darker to give more depth and contrast.

As soon as we arrived at the Straw Market, June had spotted this woman, who was busy making straw bags and embroidering scenes on them in raffia.

June was immediately inspired by her sculptured hairstyle, red-coloured top, and also by the way the dark railings behind her contrasted with the softer colours of the hats and bags at her side.

Amazingly, although this industrious lady worked all morning while I was being filmed, she still remained in exactly the same position without getting up for a break while June sketched her. You see, luck can sometimes be on your side.

THE STRAW AND RAFFIA LADY
Pen and watercolour wash on Ivorex board,
17 × 20 cm (7 × 8 in)

June sketched the scene first with a black waterproof ink pen (below left). Important shapes were the head and shoulders of the woman and the top of the railings. June didn't put anything behind these as she didn't want to spoil these shapes. She drew the hats carefully, to show their shape, but still freely and without detail.

I used watercolour first on my sketch on page 79, but June added watercolour over the top of her pen drawing here. She kept the watercolour simple and didn't overwork it.

MINUTE 3 *SKETCH*

One end of the Straw Market was covered and sectioned off into small areas for people working at a variety of different crafts.

It was decided that June should sketch the wood carver in pen as a three-minute exercise. In fact, June said afterwards that those three minutes felt agonisingly long. The hot, closed-in area, now even more crowded with cameras, lights and curious tourists – plus the feeling that so many artistic people were watching with a critical eye – made her want to do it in seconds, rather than minutes!

THE WOOD CARVER
Pen on Ivorex board, 17 × 10 cm (7 × 4 in)

June studied the wood carver while the cameras were being set up before she started her sketch. She drew the head first and shaded it in. She kept the pen on the paper all the time and the whole figure was drawn from head to foot in one continuous movement. The shape of the man's head was important and she drew this carefully. Finally, she filled in dark areas again to strengthen them.

I couldn't resist buying a straw hat in the market and wore it all day instead of my normal peaked cap. I then decided to put it on record and used it for my three-minute sketch.

I must say that, after watching June sketching the wood carver, I felt a bit of a cheat deciding to draw a simple hat for my quick sketch!

However, no matter how simple an object is, you mustn't forget to look and observe it first and decide how you are going to draw or paint it. Even if you can only see how you are going to start your sketch, once you have actually begun, the rest will happen more easily than you think.

MY STRAW HAT
2B pencil on cartridge paper, 12.5 × 15 cm (5 × 6 in)

I drew the top of the crown first, then the sides and base. When I was happy with this, I drew the brim of the hat. It was important for me to look carefully to see where the shadows fell. These are crucial on an object like this to show the contours of the shapes. The shadows on the brim give the illusion that it curves upwards, while the shadows on the top portray its domed shape where the crown of the head fits. No detail was put on the band around the hat, I just suggested the open straw work above this.

MINUTE 3 *SKETCH*

83

8

OBSERVATION

If when sketching a tree, you see that the large thick branch grows out of the trunk just beneath the broken branch, you will know exactly where to draw this branch on your paper in relation to the rest of the tree.

It is only by really observing your subject that this is possible and, in order to sketch successfully from life, you must learn how to do this. Observation is a very important skill and the more you get into the practice of really seeing things properly the better your drawing will become.

We filmed the opening to this programme at Ardastra Zoo on New Providence Island, and I explained what an artist must see when he or she observes a subject before the drawing is started. My example was a parrot's perch made from wood and tree branches and I pointed out the important elements and details that you don't see by just looking at something.

2B pencil on cartridge paper,
15 x 12.5 cm (6 × 5 in)

A SIMPLE EXERCISE

Try observing a familiar object that is near you now. Look at it carefully and let your eyes and brain dissect it. Observe its shape, size, colour, how it is made and how it sits on the table or floor. Look for small details and notice where the light is coming from. Observe the darkest areas, the lightest areas, and so on. Look hard and concentrate because, if you wanted to draw it, you would need this information to know where to put your pencil lines.

Of course, if your subject is stationary, you can do it in your own time, unlike June's birds on this page and the next!

Naturally, the more proficient you get, the faster you will be able to observe things properly. Again, this is very important when you are sketching moving objects.

To practise your powers of observation try some two-minute memory sketches. These should really help you. Look at an object for just two minutes before sketching it and see how much you can remember and draw without looking at it again.

2B pencil on cartridge paper,
29 × 40 cm (11 × 16 in)

2B pencil on cartridge paper,
10 × 10 cm (4 × 4 in)

JUNE'S PRE-FILMING SKETCHES
(mediums and sizes as shown)

When we were first looking for locations we visited the zoo to see the parrots. June did these pencil sketches in her A3 sketchbook. You can see how her confidence grew as she sketched. By drawing and observing, she was beginning to understand the anatomy and postures of the parrots better and so her hand and brain were starting to work faster. I love the two parrots sitting on perches in the sketch above. These were drawn last.

It can be very frustrating when you are sketching moving animals and birds but try to be patient and keep going.

Some of the parrots in the zoo were very tame and flew around freely in the trees. Their keeper suggested that June sketched this large macaw perched on my head, on top of my cap.

June told me later that she could hardly sketch for laughing while she did it. Indeed, it was hilarious when the macaw decided to play ring-a-roses round my hat. Then, every so often, it would stop and try to pull it off with its beak. Of course, this was an impossible task because the bird was standing on it!

This wasn't an easy subject to tackle and I think June did very well in controlling her laughter and doing the series of sketches, shown right. I think I earned Brownie points, too, since I had to put up with half an hour of the parrot's antics!

One of June's sketches from the opposite page is shown below, reproduced actual size.

FUN WITH PARROTS
2B pencil, watercolour and felt-tip pen on
cartridge paper, 28 × 35 cm (11 × 14 in)

June drew the beak and head first, as this was a very important feature. Then she drew the rest of the body but didn't put in any detail. The feathers were suggested with the brush. June used three different coloured felt-tip pens to colour some of the drawings as an experiment. She felt the colours she chose were very bright but 'fun for parrots'.

Incidentally, look at the macaw perching at June's side in the photograph (right). It didn't move a feather all the time she was drawing the moving one on my head, so she could have drawn that one many times without any problem!

June could hardly sketch because she was laughing so much!

We had great fun when we visited the Silver Cay Aquarium on Coral Island when we were filming in Nassau. This was reached by a long wooden platform stretching out into the ocean where a spiral staircase took you down inside a circular tower into an observatory under the Caribbean Sea. There were large windows all around the wall with amazing views of the ocean and many different species of fish and marine life in their natural habitat. Actually, from their point of view, I'm sure we humans were the ones in the fish tank!

While the cameras were being set up, I observed the fish and watched one species in particular, as they seemed to be staying in a shoal in front of my window longer than any of the others. So I decided to start with them and, by the time the cameras were ready, I felt I knew these fish a little better.

LIFE UNDER THE OCEAN
(mediums and sizes as shown)

I had observed the head of the fish (below, top left) very carefully as this helped me to familiarize myself with its characteristics. I started, as always, with the head, then 'felt' the shape of the fish as I drew a line down to its tail. After I had drawn a few, I began to understand them and my pencil was working well. However, the daylight was going so I decided not to draw any more and started adding watercolour very simply. I also painted a suggestion of the water.

Before the light went, I had time to draw some more fish using a biro (right). As with a pencil, I achieved dark lines by putting pressure on and lighter lines by using less pressure.

Finally, I saw the lobster (below right), silhouetted against the darkening sea and sketched it while the cameras were being dismantled. I started with the head and my 2B pencil was continually on the move until it was completed (in about five minutes). Notice how freely the shading was done.

2B pencil and watercolour
on cartridge paper,
17 x 23 cm (7 x 9 in)

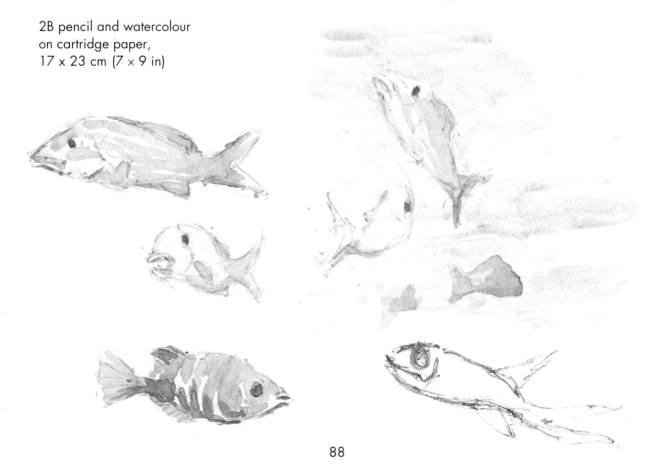

88

Biro on cartridge paper,
12.5 × 23 cm (5 × 9 in)

2B pencil on cartridge paper, 23 × 33 cm (9 × 13 in)

USING CONTÉ CRAYONS

Conté sketching crayons have been used by artists for centuries. I used Black and Sanguine (a red colour) for my sketches. You can buy these crayons individually or in boxes of mixed colours and there are 72 shades to choose from. These crayons don't come off on your fingers like pastels or charcoal.

I had decided to draw these two iguanas in conté crayon for a three-minute sketch. After the fast-moving fish, I thought it would be relatively easy – but one should never take anything for granted! These creatures can move surprisingly quickly, changing their attitude in a second. Luckily, the lower one, which I drew in red crayon, was asleep and this made things easier!

IGUANAS
Conté crayon on cartridge paper, 17 × 25 cm (7 × 10 in)

With each iguana, I used the edge of the crayon to draw the outline, drawing the head first and then working down to the tail. The shading was done with the flat end of the crayon and I didn't attempt to sketch any background.

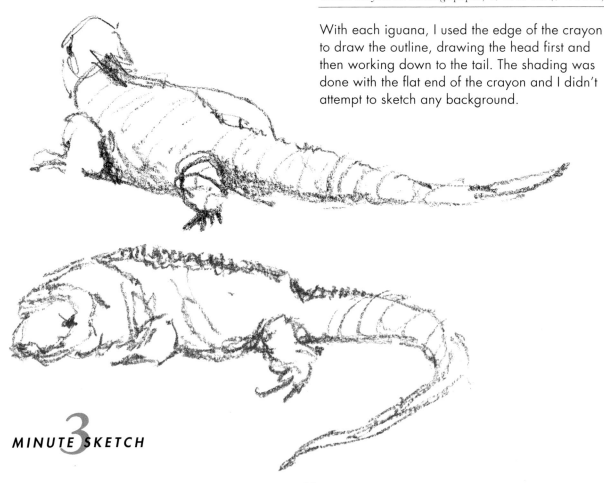

MINUTE 3 *SKETCH*

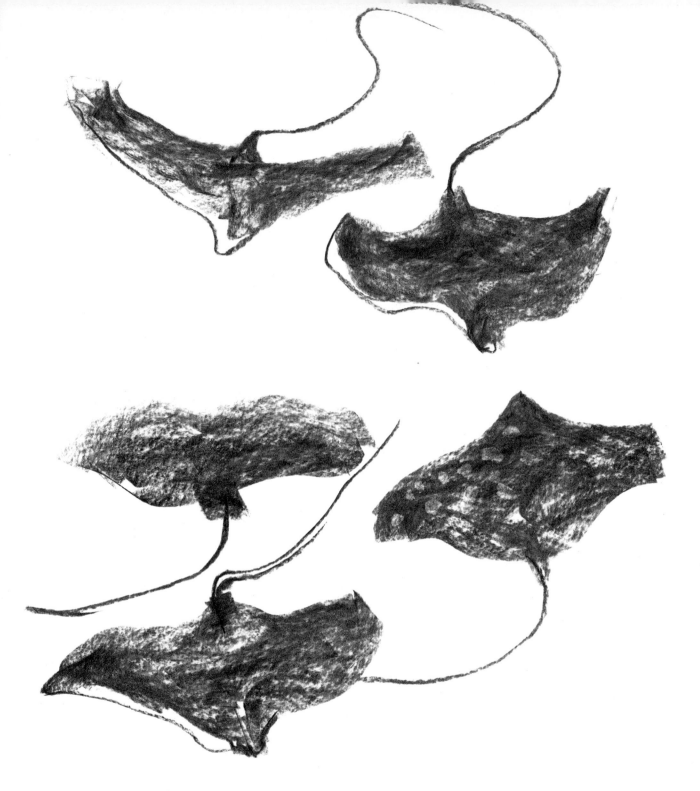

STINGRAYS
Charcoal on cartridge paper,
43 × 25 cm (17 × 10 in)

June drew some stingrays which were swimming in a very large open air aquarium. Sketched in charcoal, I think these are real beauties. It is an ideal medium for this kind of subject.

Naturally, speed was essential because these creatures move fast, so June used the long edge of the charcoal stick for the wings. The end of the charcoal was used for the tail and the front edge, where this showed.

June didn't do any finger smudging but used a putty eraser to lightly rub out some markings on the stingray, centre right.

June wanted to sketch some of the children on Harbour Island and so we found a spot on Bay Street near the sea where they play after school. The only possible place for June to work from was the road, because of the positioning of the cameras.

One of the joys of sketching is being able to find an out-of-the-way corner and work without interruption or discomfort. However, to accommodate two cameras and work within sound recording restrictions for television, June and I often found ourselves in rather uncomfortable sketching positions!

Normally there are no such problems. When you find a sketching spot, always sit to work if you can because you will then have much more control over your pencil. It's also much more comfortable! June was standing to draw these children for the cameras and you can't get the same pressure on your pencil in this position. This means that the dark areas in her sketch are grey, and not 'black'.

There were just three or four children when we arrived but by the time the cameras were ready the whole area was swarming with potential television stars!

SCHOOL CHILDREN
2B pencil on cartridge paper, 25 × 7.5 cm (10 × 3 in)

After June had finished the three-minute sketch on the next page, she sat down to draw these children while the crew were packing up the cameras. She could put more pressure on her pencil because she was resting the sketchpad on her knees, so her pencil lines are much stronger.

JUST SITTING AROUND
2B pencil on cartridge paper, actual size

June decided the head, legs and arms were the
most important features to concentrate on, to
show the attitude of the children. The clothes
were not tonally important and she left them
unshaded. When one child moved, June drew
another one.

MINUTE 3 SKETCH

9

PASTEL TECHNIQUES

It is always good to experiment with different mediums as this helps you to think differently and stops you getting into a rut. Pastels are a colourful medium that can produce fantastic results and they are ideal for sketching. Although I must confess I feel more at home with a brush than a pastel stick, I always get excited and inspired whenever I use them. June feels the same way but I feel she has a closer affinity with pastels than I do.

There are two ranges of artists' quality pastels. The classic round soft pastel comes wrapped in a very thin paper tube. You need to discard this before working with it. By the way, you will usually work with small pieces so don't worry if your pastels break. Artists' Square Pastels, which come unwrapped, have a firmer consistency and are ideal for detailed line work as well as for producing broad flat areas of colour.

June and I took boxes of Daler-Rowney's 36 assorted soft pastels and 48 assorted square pastels with us for filming. We only used a few of these colours but it is good to have plenty available – you can't colour mix pastels from three primaries as you can with watercolour.

The best paper to work on for pastels is Ingres paper, which is available in a selection of colours. You can buy this as single sheets, sketchpads or boards. Use a kneadable putty eraser if you want to rub out any pastel as you work. To make it easier to find my colours when I work, I use the partitioned box shown below. The partitions were cut from card and taped into a standard pastel cardboard box.

I advise you to fix your pastel work when you have finished a sketch. The fixative Perfix can be used for pastels, pencil and charcoal and is sold in an ozone-friendly aerosol.

Our selection of pastels (above), and pastel scribbles on tinted Ingres papers and cartridge paper (right).

I couldn't wait to sip this cocktail but I had to sketch it first!

At Compass Point Hotel, one of the hotels we stayed at during the filming of the television series, the barman made up an exotic cocktail, for me to paint. It looked gorgeous in the sunlight.

As luck would have it, the boxes of pastels we had brought with us didn't include a colour that was anywhere near the cocktail's unusual hue. However, although you can try mixing the correct colour on paper, it won't spoil your sketch if you use the nearest colour in your selection.

COMPASS POINT COCKTAIL
Pastel on Ingres paper, 33 × 23 cm (13 × 9 in)

I drew the ellipse of the top of the glass first using the edge of a hard pastel, then I drew in the rest of the glass. I then changed to soft pastels and used single strokes of greens and blues for the liquid contents of the glass, leaving some background paper showing through to suggest reflected highlights from the background colour.

Notice that I painted the lemons and the straw darker inside the glass and simple, single pastel strokes were used to suggest the umbrella and palm tree.

Finally, I used white pastel for the highlights on the glass and decided to paint a bright pink background last as a design feature. Of course, if there had really been a pink background, this colour would have been reflected in the glass.

June had decided to paint some pieces of fruit in pastels for this programme but when this exotic and colourful fruit arrangement was brought out to the table, she decided to sketch the whole thing. She particularly liked the scarlet hibiscus flowers decorating each end of the bowl.

FRUIT AND HIBISCUS
Pastel on Ingres paper, 23 × 33 cm (9 × 13 in)

June did the drawing with black pastel and then filled in with the bright colours, blending some together in places with her fingers. The green pineapple leaves and the hibiscus flowers were drawn in boldly with single colours. The shadow areas on the bowl and the table were kept dark to contrast with the bright areas, helping to suggest strong sunlight. Finally, June used black pastel to draw around some areas of the finished painting to give extra dimension and shape.

The object of my three-minute sketch (below) was to pick out a subject from a larger and more complicated scene. I chose to sketch the yacht moorings on Harbour Island and chose a moored cruiser as my subject. I made sure I sketched in the jetty on the left, which was nearer to me than the cruiser. This added more interest to the sketch and helped give the illusion of distance.

For her three-minute pastel sketch on the next page, June chose a hibiscus in full bloom. The colour of these flowers is truly magnificent.

MINUTE **3** *SKETCH*

YACHT MOORINGS
2B pencil on cartridge paper, 10 × 25 cm (4 × 10 in)

I blunted the point on my pencil and this helped to shade in and cover the area more quickly. The boat was the important object and I did this first. The mooring/jetty posts were also very important as they established the cruiser's environment. I didn't try to be too accurate with these but I did look at the scene with screwed-up eyes, which showed me the important posts as dark shapes. I also added simple reflections which were important to give the impression of water.

3
MINUTE SKETCH

HIBISCUS
Pastel on Ingres paper, 28 × 25 cm (11 × 12 in)

June drew the flower very freely first using dark blue pastel. Then she coloured in the red petals using the long edge of her pastel stick. The leaves and background were also drawn mainly with a long edge to enable areas to be covered very quickly. This also stopped the sketch becoming too detailed or fussy.

Finally, June added some very free white pastel strokes at the top of the sketch which helped to give a lovely feelng of light and life to the picture.

10

ENJOYMENT SKETCHES

While looking for locations, June and I saw some scenes that we felt we just had to sketch. We decided to do these in the last programme, which would concentrate on enjoyment sketches.

I had previously seen and felt inspired by an old ocean-going tug moored in Nassau Harbour. We checked to make sure it would still be there and the answer was 'yes'. However, on the day of filming we were devastated to find an empty quay! Eventually, I found a different tug to sketch but, just as the cameras were ready and I was about to start work, a pleasure cruiser anchored directly in front of me, totally blocking my view. It definitely was not my day!

David, the producer, disappeared to use his negotiating skills and the boat kindly moved away to moor in another area. I was finally ready to begin, even if it was with a different tug and two hours behind schedule! But I enjoyed every minute of it.

THE COLOURFUL TUG
2B pencil and watercolour on cartridge paper,
33 × 28 cm (13 × 11 in)

I started by drawing the line of the deck and the vertical line for the bows. I then put in the cabins and superstructure, working up from deck level. Finally, I drew the bottom of the boat resting in the water. A man walked past the boat on the quay and I drew him in to give scale.

Once I had finished my pencil sketch (left), I began painting, starting with the cabins and superstructure. When this was dry, I added the blue on the cabin and the green around the hull. Then I painted the light blue of the ropes on the bows and, when these were dry, I painted the dark hull (leaving white paper for the water being pumped out of the hull) and then the tyres.

Finally, I painted the sea, and also added dark accents over the painting where I felt it needed them.

June spotted the Library from Parliament Square in Nassau and thought it looked very colourful with people sitting and standing in groups on the steps leading up to the doorway. She really wanted to paint this eye-catching scene.

On the day we arrived for filming, the steps were bare and nobody was there! Even by the time our cameras were ready, the steps were still unpopulated, so David disappeared with his producer's cap on and, five minutes later, as if by magic, we had people on the steps and June could start work. After filming, June sketched some figures in pen (below) while she waited for the crew to pack up their equipment.

THE LIBRARY STEPS, NASSAU
2B pencil and watercolour on cartridge paper,
20 × 17 cm (8 × 7 in)

After drawing the scene in pencil, June painted in the pink wall, the steps and the green shrubs. She added colour to the figures and painted the light-coloured trunks of the two palm trees on the right. When this was dry she painted the dark palm tree and finished the figures. Notice the dark doorway – this helps to emphasize the two light-coloured figures (light against dark).

You can see how unlaboured this sketch is, yet it still tells a story.

Pen on cartridge paper, 11 × 25 cm (4½ × 10 in)

Fisherman's Dock really inspired me.

I finally got the chance to sketch it for television.

Of all the fabulous scenes that we saw while we were filming, Fisherman's Dock on Harbour Island was the one that inspired me the most. From an artistic point of view, it was definitely my favourite spot on the whole island.

Even in the mornings when it was deserted the dock made an interesting scene to sketch, but during the afternoon, when the fishermen came back in their boats and unloaded their catch, the jetty became a hive of activity.

During our stay on Harbour Island, I saw this scene from many different viewpoints and in a variety of weather conditions. I know I could have stayed on the island for a month, just sketching and painting this scene in all its different moods, and never become tired of it.

FISHERMAN'S DOCK, HARBOUR ISLAND
2B pencil on cartridge paper, 10 × 33 cm (4 × 13 in)

I established the top of the jetty first, then started drawing from the end of it, working towards the covered area at the land end on the right of the sketch. If a fisherman went into a position that I liked as I worked, I stopped what I was drawing and put him into the sketch. When sketching activity like this, you can pick and choose where you place your people.

The fishermen's boats were important as they broke up the water line of the jetty. In real life, the tallest post and the dark one at the end of the jetty were smaller than I drew them – they only came up to the horizon and looked as if they were holding it up! So I made them taller, which I felt helped the composition.

I only put enough simple reflections to give the impression of water. If I had put a lot of work into the sea, the jetty would have lost some of its importance in the sketch.

The photograph (above) shows the view from our hotel on Harbour Island. Isn't it idyllic? It isn't surprising that it was one of June's favourite painting spots. She wanted to sketch it for television but every time it was planned into our schedule gale force winds made it impossible to film her doing this for television.

However, on the very last afternoon of filming, luck was on our side. The winds finally calmed down and June was able to get her wish at last. She was filmed for television doing her sketch (shown on the next page) and enjoyed every minute of it.

CORAL SANDS, HARBOUR ISLAND
2B pencil and watercolour on cartridge paper,
35 × 28 cm (14 × 11 in)

June drew the two palm trees first, starting with the one on the left, then she established the horizon and the line of the beach.

The sky was painted a very pale French Ultramarine. Then June painted the dark blue sea, the turquoise sea and finally the beach. She let the beach colour continue to the bottom of the sketch and, when this was dry, painted in the trunks, then the leaves and finally the foreground.

June introducing her painting spot for television.

SKETCHING & DRAWING 20 TIPS

1 Always carry a sketchpad, pencil and eraser with you so that you can make the most of every sketching opportunity.

2 Never worry about using an eraser – it is an essential part of your sketching kit.

3 Whatever medium you are using, keep your equipment to a minimum if you are going to sketch outdoors.

4 Don't keep looking around the next corner – sketch the first subject that inspires you.

5 Always make sure that you are sitting or standing comfortably when you sketch.

6 When sketching with pencil, you can create dark and light lines by varying the amount of pressure you put on the lead.

7 Remember that you are trying to create an impression of the scene you are sketching.

8 Don't be too fussy or you will lose the atmosphere of your sketch.

9 When sketching buildings, remember to establish your eye-level first.

10 If anything is above your eye level, you will be able to see underneath it, and if anything is below your eye level, you will be able to see on top of it.

18 Don't worry if you haven't finished the complete person, or animal, before they move away. Start sketching another one.

19 The more you sketch a subject, the more you will begin to understand it.

20 Above all, remember that sketching is fun, so enjoy it!

11 Make a note of the sun's position (your light source) on information sketches in case you wish to work from them later at home.

12 When sketching with watercolour, leave plenty of white paper showing through to add sparkle to your picture.

13 Pastel and charcoal sketches can easily become smudged, so take care while working and always fix your finished sketches.

14 When sketching moving objects, your pencil or pen must move quickly. This only comes with practice.

15 Don't forget to do plenty of three-minute sketches. They are a very useful exercise.

16 Remember to test your powers of observation by doing two-minute memory sketches as well!

17 When sketching people or animals, always study them carefully first before you start work.

BAHAMAS
Sketchbook

Angela's house, Nassau

In the air! The captain of our British Caledonian DC10 aeroplane

The band at
the Atlantis Hotel

The t-shirt lady

Alwyn at the Straw Market

Alwyn's 5 minute break!

The TV crew, Nassau

Scotty filming Alwyn
working on his oil sketch
of Harbour Island

Big Red's boat, Harbour Island

From the Harbour Lounge bar, Harbour Island

When I returned to
sketch this boat for
TV a few days later,
it had gone!

The Big Fig tree, Bay Street (a meeting place on Harbour Island)

children, Harbour Island

The day of the storm!

Birds, Harbour Island

Workmen, Nassau

I was told this was Raymond's
House, Harbour Island

The ice man, Bay Street,
Harbour Island

The water taxi, Harbour Island

Palms and power poles, Harbour Island

On the beach,
Harbour Island

ON THE FILM SET

During the making of the television series, Liam, one of the members of the film crew, took some photographs for this book, and June and I also had our cameras ready when we weren't busy being filmed. These photographs were mainly taken as 'candid camera' shots to capture special moments before and during filming.

Our schedule was extremely demanding and our working days started early and finished late. However, with the friendliness of the Bahamian people, the colour and beauty of their country and, in particular, the help of the Bahamas Tourist Office, we thoroughly enjoyed every minute of our stay.

As usual, the sense of humour of the crew (especially that of Scotty, our chief cameraman) gave us some magic moments, too. We now have an album full of photographs to bring back wonderful memories and I hope you will enjoy sharing a few of them with us.

Above: 'Shall we give this the thumbs up?'

Below: Anything for television!

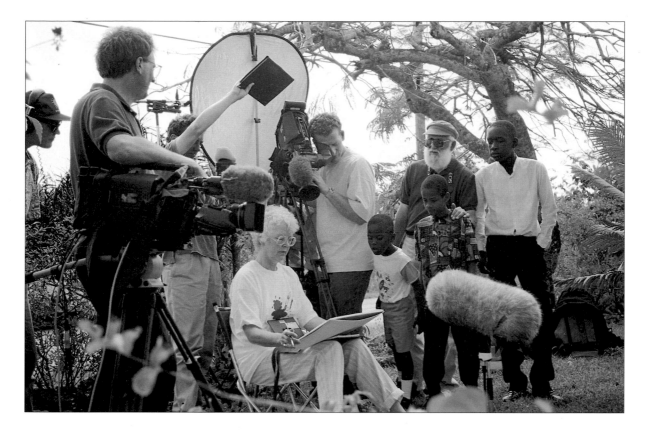

Who says painting is relaxing?

'Don't step back, Scotty!'

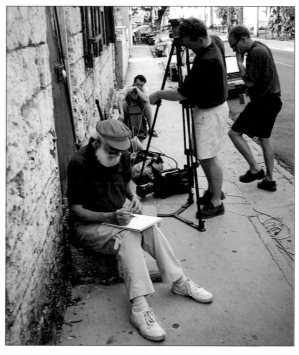

The Bahamian pavement artist.

'Oh, come on, David, it's that shape!'

June in the hot seat.

'Don't laugh at my new hat!'

'There's no other way, David!'

Getting the bird!

'You can take June's place if you want to – over there in five minutes!'

'Take 6...take 7...take 8...I'll get it right one day!'

What an idyllic setting for a working lunch!

'You said that when I'd sketched the cocktail, I could drink it!'

BAHAMAS FACTFILE

During the making of the television series *Crawshaw's Sketching and Drawing Course*, we stayed on just two of the many islands of the Bahamas: New Providence Island and Harbour Island. (NPI indicates New Providence Island and HI indicates Harbour Island.) We flew there with Caledonian Airways and our travel arrangements were made by Golden Lion Travel Ltd, Caledonian House, Perimeter Road South, Gatwick, West Sussex RH8 OLF. Internal flights between the islands were provided by Bahamasair.

We stayed at the following hotels: Compass Point, Love Beach, Nassau (NPI); Coral Sands Hotel, North Eleuthera (HI); Atlantis Resort and Casino, Paradise Island, Nassau (NPI); The Marriott, Cable Beach, Nassau (NPI).

We have listed the locations we used by programme order (below). If you ever visit the Bahamas, we hope this information will be helpful to you.

If you would like further information and travel advice about the Bahamas, write to the Bahamas Tourist Office, 3 The Billings, Walnut Tree Close, Guildford, Surrey GU1 4UL.

PROGRAMME 1 Compass Point Hotel (NPI); Arawak Cay (NPI)

PROGRAMME 2 Coral Sands Hotel (HI); St James' Church, Adelaide Village (NPI); Dunmore Town (HI); Coral Sands Hotel (HI)

PROGRAMME 3 Coral Sands Hotel (HI); Parliament Street, Nassau (NPI); Atlantis Hotel (NPI); Coral Sands Hotel (HI)

PROGRAMME 4 Dunmore Town (HI); Coral Sands Hotel (HI)

PROGRAMME 5 Dunmore Town (HI); Coral Sands Hotel (HI)

PROGRAMME 6 Government House, Nassau (NPI); Ardastra Gardens and Zoo (NPI); Parliament Street, Nassau (NPI); St James' Church, Adelaide Village (NPI)

PROGRAMME 7 Straw Market, Nassau (NPI); Compass Point Hotel (NPI)

PROGRAMME 8 Ardastra Gardens and Zoo (NPI); Coral Island (NPI); Dunmore Town (HI)

PROGRAMME 9 Compass Point Hotel (NPI)

PROGRAMME 10 Prince George Wharf, Nassau (NPI); Public Library, Nassau (NPI); Dunmore Town (HI); Coral Sands Hotel (HI)